Science for All

Book 3

For Class 3

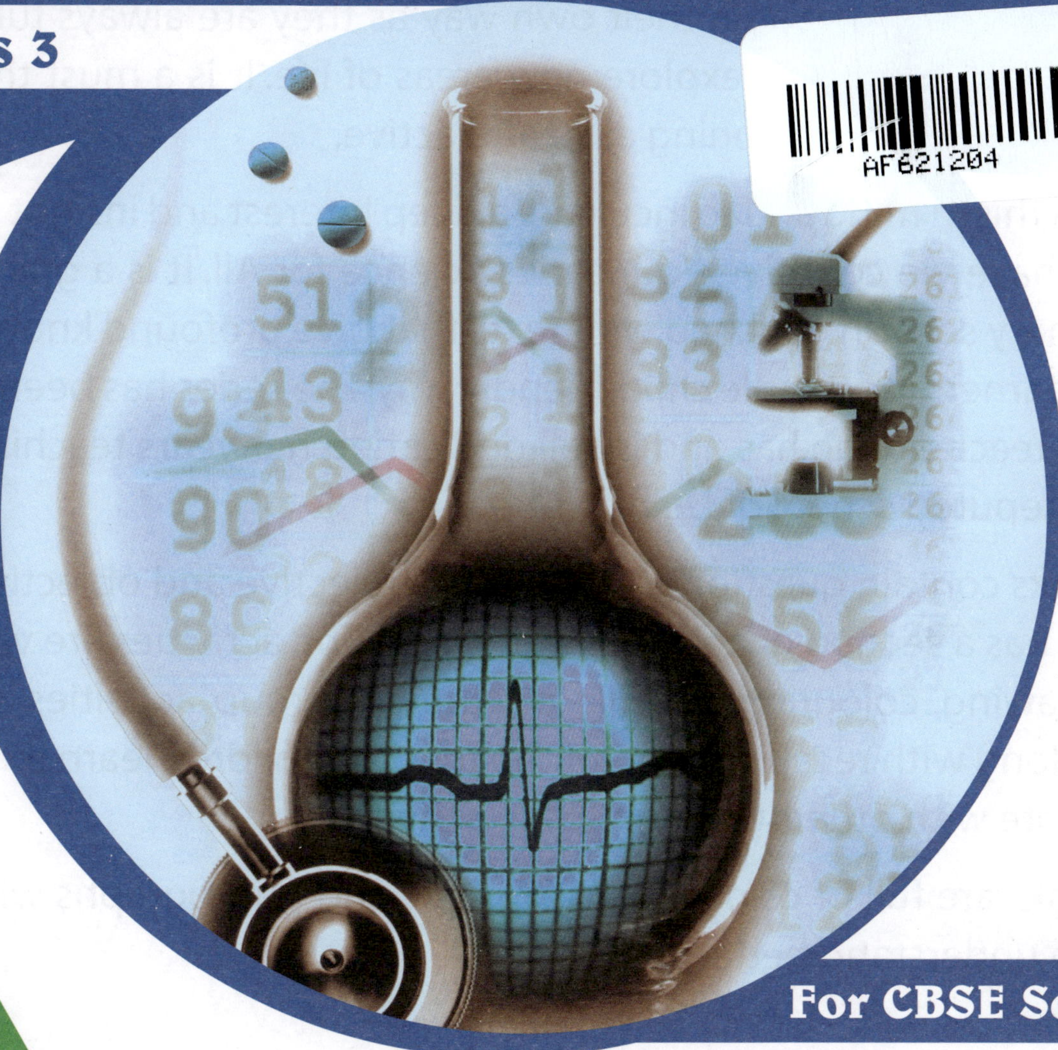

For CBSE Schools

Based on CCE

Ruchi Arora

Pegasus

Preface

Science today has ceased to be just a subject which is limited to books only. It has become a way of life. In every walk of life we require science; we need it to drive a car, watch television, click a photograph or even when light up our room! Science is actually knowledge that pervades nature on the whole.

Every child is a scientist in their own way as they are always full of curiosity and are always ready to explore new areas of life. It is a must that we elders keep this spirit of questioning alive and active.

Keeping this in mind and to inculcate a deep interest and insight into this very subject have we conceived our series Science for All. It is a graded series for the primary section enriched with texts that give profound knowledge to the young learners in a simple child-friendly way. The series has been authored by a senior teacher who has and is still dedicating her years teaching Science in a much reputed school of Delhi.

The books contain questions of all types, subjective and objective both. Each chapter has a section of activities at the end. The activities are varied ranging from drawing, colouring, pasting pictures to group activities and pair and share. Along with recapitulation of the text, the children learn to research and co-operate with others through these activities.

The books are full of colourful illustrations and photographs which help the children understand better.

From the author

Science has become a way of life today whether one has to connect to the world by using the internet or light a bulb. Our day to day activities are governed by the principles of science knowingly or unknowingly. Scientific bent of mind is a judicious way to deal with the small obstacles that governs our everyday life.

The series **Science for All** is prepared in accordance with the new syllabus prescribed by NCERT on the basis of CCE (Continuous and Comprehensive Evaluation). CCE emphasizes on the continuous learning by different methods to develop creativity, reasoning, analytical and thinking abilities in the learner.

In this series, we have emphasized on the learning of science through simple activities and observations. The books are related to the immediate environment of a child and explain everything that he sees in the light of scientific knowledge. This will facilitate better understanding of the facts of science. The books are written in simple and child friendly language with lots of illustrations and activities that the child will enjoy doing. This will enhance the participation of the learners; in other words encourage 'learning by doing'. It will stimulate the learner's thinking and scientific temper and encourage the overall development and holistic personality of the child.

The exercises given at the end of each lesson contains the questions of both types as per CCE norms, i.e. related to Formative Assessment and Summative Assessment. This will make their concept more clear and inspire them to apply their knowledge every moment. The group activities will enhance group learning and social interaction of the child.

Ruchi Arora

Contents

1 Animals and their Feeding Habits

Like us, animals also need food to live. Food helps them to grow and stay healthy. Food gives them energy. Animals need energy to move about. They need energy to hunt or gather food.

Animals cannot prepare their own food. All animals depend on plants and other animals for their food. Animals can be divided into three groups depending upon their feeding habits.

Plant eating animals

Some animals eat grass or green plants and they are called plant eating animals. Such animals are also called **herbivores**. Cows, buffaloes, deer, goats, sheep, zebras, giraffes etc are examples of such animals.

Herbivores

Flesh eating animals

Some animals like lion, tiger, foxes, leopards eat the flesh of other animals. They are flesh eating animals. Flesh eating animals are called **carnivores**.

Carnivores

Some animals feed on flesh of dead animals like vultures, hyenas and jackals. Such animals are called **scavengers**.

Scavengers

Plant and flesh eating animals

Some animals eat both plants and the flesh of other animals. Such animals are known as **omnivores**. They eat different parts of plants according to their need. And from animals, they get food in the form of milk, eggs, fish and meat. Animals like crows, cats and bears are omnivores. Humans are omnivores too.

Omnivores

Insect eating animals

Some animals live by eating insects like frogs, lizards, snakes, birds and fishes.

Parasites

Parasites are living organisms that live on or in the body of other organism. They obtain their food from the body of the host in which they live. Tapeworm and roundworm are the example of parasites.

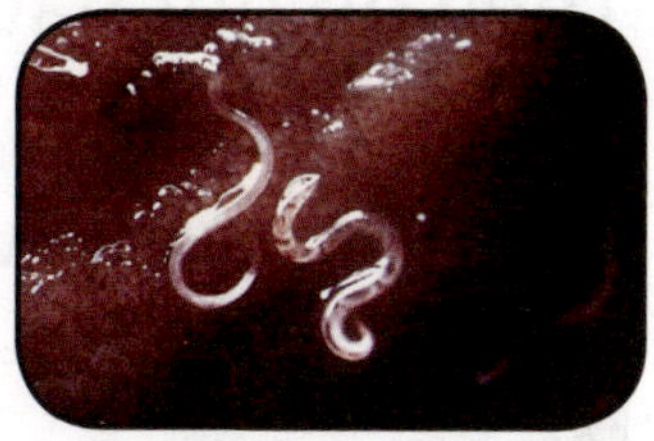

Tapeworm

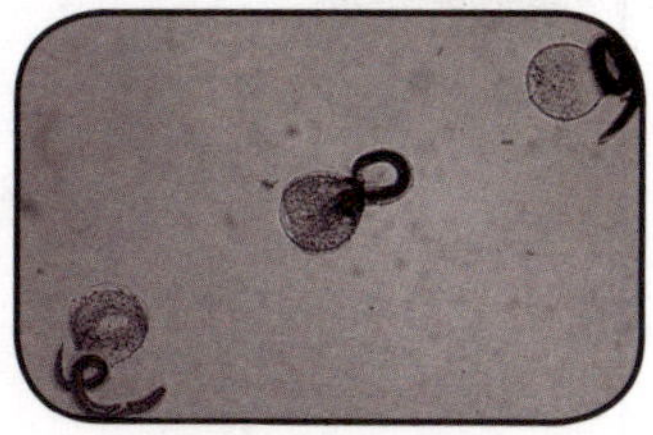

Roundworm

Food chain

Food chain is the dependence of one group of animals on another to get food. For example a deer eats grass and a lion eats the deer. This forms a chain which is called a **food chain**. All food chains begin from plants.

Food Chain

Ways of feeding

Different animals eat different types of food. The kind of food they eat depends on the shape of their mouth, jaws and teeth.

Swallowing

Some animals like frog, lizard and snake do not bite or chew the food. They do not have teeth. The lizard and frog have a long sticky tongue to catch insects. Snakes swallow their food. They can open their mouth wide to swallow animals that are bigger than them.

Frog swallowing an insect

Snake swallowing a frog

Gnawing

'Gnaw' means to bite something repeatedly. Animals like rabbit, squirrel and rat have sharp front chisel like teeth. With these teeth they can bite hard, rough foods like grains, nuts, fruits and seeds.

Rat

Rabbit

Squirrel

Chewing the cud

Some animals like cows, buffaloes, sheep and camel first swallow their food without chewing it. Later they bring it back into their mouth and chew it with their grinding teeth. This is called **chewing the cud**.

Cow

Camel

Sheep

Tearing and chewing the flesh

Animals like lion, tiger, foxes, dogs have very sharp, pointed teeth. With these teeth they tear the flesh. They have strong, broad and flat back teeth. These help them to chew flesh and bones.

Feeding habits of some other animals

Insects like butterflies, bees, mosquitoes have long, thin tube like structures to suck food.

Mosquito

Butterfly

Bee

An elephant uses its trunk to eat and drink. It uses its trunk to uproot grass and tear leaves from trees and push them into its mouth. It also sucks water with its trunk and shoots it into the mouth. It uses its trunk to have a shower also!

Elephant

Dog

Cat

Earthworm

Animals like cats and dogs lap water and milk with their tongue.

An Earthworm swallows soil which has dead plants and animals in it.

Care of animals

Animals are our friends. All animals need protection and care. Killing the animals is a punishable offence under the wild life protection Act. We should take good care of our pets and domestic animals. We should provide good food and clean shelter and try to give them a healthy life.

Do yourself

A. Find the odd one out in the group.

Herbivores

Cow	Deer	Leopard	Goat

Carnivores

Lion	Tiger	Leopards	Zebra

Omnivores

Giraffe	Crow	Man	Bear

Gnawing animals

Rat	Squirrel	Lizard	Rabbit

Animals that chew the cud

Cow	Buffalo	Camel	Monkey

B. Unscramble the letters with the help of clues.

1. Animal that swallow food NSKAE ____________
2. Animal having chisel like teeth BARBTI ____________
3. Animal that chew the cud AMCLE ____________
4. Animal that sucks blood OSMUQTIO ____________

C. Tick (✓) the correct answer.

1. An elephant sucks water with its:

   a. Trunk ☐

   b. Tail ☐

c. Teeth ☐

2. Bears are called

   a. Omnivores ☐

   b. Carnivores ☐

   c. Herbivores ☐

3. A butterfly sucks nectar with the help of

   a. Trunk ☐

   b. Tongue ☐

   c. Sucking tube ☐

4. A giraffe to reach the top of tall trees uses it's

   a. Tongue ☐

   b. Neck ☐

   c. Trunk ☐

5. It has sharp pointed teeth to tear the flesh

   a. Lion ☐

   b. Horses ☐

   c. Zebra ☐

D. Answer the following questions.

1. What are herbivorous animals? Name any two such animals.
2. What are omnivorous animals? Name any two of them.
3. What do you understand by chewing the cud? Name two animals that chew the cud.

4. What is the food chain? Form a food chain with the following—frog, grass, snake and grasshopper.

5. How does an earthworm have its food?

E. Write the names of the animals which you see below.

Pick up their first letter and write it down in the box given. Now read the new word and see what it is. Now write the first letter. One has been done for you.

F. Visit a park or a zoo and observe the animals there carefully. Name them in the spaces given below.

On the tree ____________________ ____________________

On the ground ____________________ ____________________

In the cage ____________________ ____________________

In the water ____________________ ____________________

G. Match the following

Sharp front teeth

Broad back teeth

Sharp pointed curved front teeth

Hollow tube

Sticky tongue

H. Jumbo the elephant wants to take a shower on a hot day. Help him reach the pond.

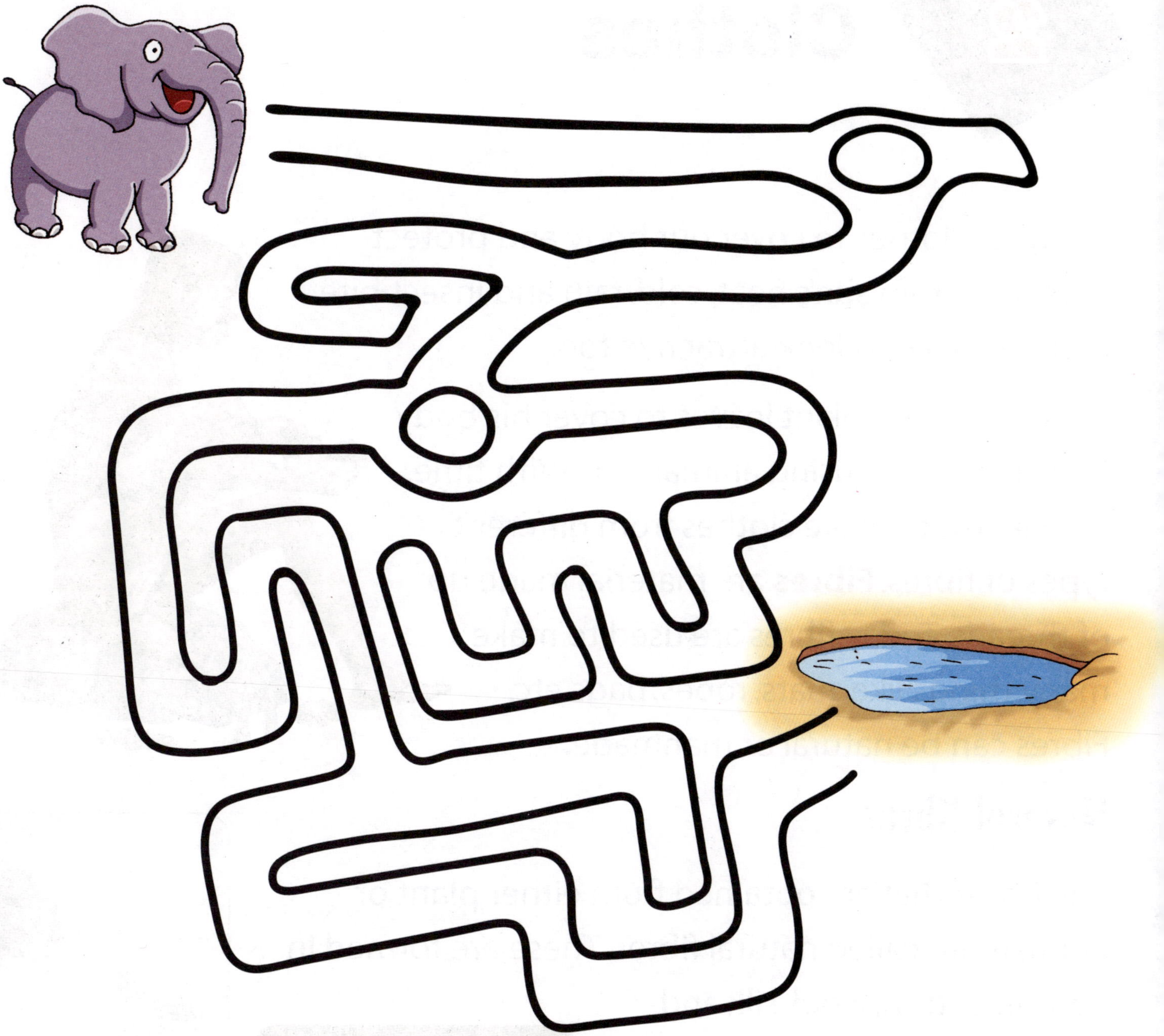

Activity time

Collect the pictures of at least six animals. Paste them in your scrapbook and write about their eating habits.

2 Clothes

We wear clothes to cover our body and protect ourselves from sun's heat, cold, rain and insect bite. Clothes make us look attractive too.

Early man used plant leaves to cover his body. Later he started using animal skin. With time, man learnt to make clothes from different types of fibres. **Fibres** are material made up of threads. Today fibres are used to make many things like, mats, ropes, bags etc. Fibres can be natural or manmade.

Natural fibres

The fibres that are obtained from either plant or animals are called natural fibres. These are formed in nature. Cotton, wool, silk and jute are **natural fibres**.

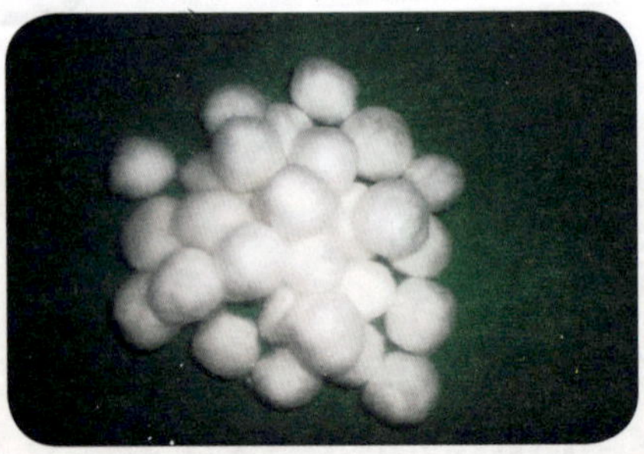

Cotton

Cotton Clothes

Cotton

We get cotton from cotton plants. Fine threads of cotton are made from cotton flower. These threads are then used to weave beautiful clothes of cotton.

Wool

Sweater

We get wool from sheep and hair of rabbits. Wool is woven into woollen clothes and woollen clothes keep our body warm during winter. They have air spaces between them which do not allow heat of our body to go out. Thus they make us feel warm.

Sheep

Wool

Silkworm

Silk

We get silk from cocoons of silkworms. Silk worms feed on mulberry leaves. Silk thread is very fine in nature.

Jute

Jute is a natural fibre that we get from jute plant, apart from clothes, jute is also used to make ropes, jute bags etc.

Jute Proudcts

Man-made fibres

Fibres that are made by man are called **man-made** fibres. They are also called **synthetic fibres**. Nylon, rayon, polyester, terry cotton are some man-made fibres.

Nylon Fabric

Nylon Rope

Terry Cotton

Clothes and climate

We wear clothes made of different materials according to the climate of the place where we live.

If we live in a hot place, we wear cotton clothes. They keep our body cool. When it is cold, we wear woollen and silk clothes. They keep our body warm. In very cold places when it snows, people wear clothes made of fur to keep themselves warm.

When it rains, we use raincoats, gumboots made of waterproof materials.

Summer Clothes

Winter Clothes

Rainy Season Clothes

Clothes and occasions

We wear clothes according to the occasions like party, marriage or an athletic events etc.

Marriage

Athletic Event

Clothes and country

People from different countries wear different types of clothes.

Indian

European

Arabian

Japanese

Clothes and work

People wear clothes according to the work they do. Such clothes are called **uniform**.

Nurse

Policeman

Doctor

Astronaut

Do Yourself

A. Write (T) for true statements and (F) for false statements

1. Early man used leaves to cover their bodies. ☐
2. We get wool from silkworm. ☐
3. Nylon is a natural fibre. ☐
4. Cotton clothes keep us warm during winter. ☐
5. We look smart in clean and ironed clothes. ☐
6. We wear a swimsuit while jogging. ☐

B. Answer the following questions.

1. Why do we wear clothes?
2. What are natural fibres?
3. Write the name of any two man-made fibres.
4. Write the name of any two things made from jute.

C. Write the names of the persons who wear the following uniform.

________ ________ ________ ________

D. Write what kind of fibres we get from the following.

______________ ______________ ______________

E. Is there anything wrong with the pictures? If yes, put a cross on the wrong pictures.

Activity time

Collect pictures of men and women from different parts of India wearing their traditional dress and paste the pictures in the scrapbook. Also write to which part of India they belong.

3 Soil

Soil is the top layer of the Earth. The plants grow in the soil. Plants take water and mineral from the soil with their roots. A root fixes the plant in the soil. Soil is necessary for the growth of plants. Plants take water and minerals from the soil with the help of their roots. A root fixes the plant in the soil. Soil is necessary for the growth of plants.

Formation of soil

Soil is not formed in a day. Long ago when there was no life on Earth, it was covered with huge rocks. These rocks broke up into smaller pieces due to the action of rain, wind and sun's heat. This continued for millions of years. These small pieces broke down further into smaller pieces. Dead plants and animals also got mixed with these tiny rock pieces. Finally, these tiny particles could not break further and formed soil.

The colour and texture of soil is not the same everywhere. We have different colours and different types of texture in soil. Some soil maybe light brown in colour while others maybe dark brown or even red. By touching a soil with our hands we can feel the texture of it; it maybe

Particles of Soil

gritty or sticky or may feel like flour. Different types of soil have particles of different sizes.

Layers of soil

Soils have a number of layers. This can be seen by this activity.

ACTIVITY 1

Dig some soil from a garden. Add it in an empty glass jar. Add water in it. Mix it well and cover the jar. Allow the mixture to stand for at least half an hour. Now look at the jar carefully. You will see the layers being formed in the jar.

The bottom layer consists of stones. Above it is a layer of sand. The clay settles above the sand. Then there is a layer of muddy water.

On the top of the water there are dead leaves and insects floating in it. This is called **humus**. It makes the soil fertile.

Soil contains water

All types of soil contain water. The water contained in the soil is called **moisture**. Plants absorb this water from the soil. Let us see this through an activity.

ACTIVITY 2

Take some soil in a container and cover with a lid. Heat the container on a low flame with the help of an adult. Open the lid a little later. You will see tiny drops of water on the lid. This shows that soil has moisture in it.

Soil contains air

Soil contains air also. This can be seen through this activity.

ACTIVITY 3

Collect some soil in a glass jar. Pour water over it and you will see air bubbles forming as you pour the water. This shows that soil contains air that escapes in the form of bubbles.

Apart from water and air, soil also contains minerals. Minerals are materials that make the soil fertile. Soil can be made rich by adding manure. Manure is the waste got from animals and plants that is mixed with the soil. It helps the plants to grow well.

Types of soil

Sandy soil, clay soil and loamy soil are the three main types of soil.

Sandy soil

The particles of sandy soil are big in size. It is a light and dry soil. It cannot hold much water. It feels gritty when touched.

Clay soil

Clay particles are very fine in nature. This type of soil can hold a lot of water. It feels sticky when touched. Clay is mostly used for making pots and toys.

Loamy soil

It is a mixture of sandy and clay soils. It can hold both air and water. It has a lot of humus. Loamy is the best soil for plants to grow.

Uses of soil

1. Soil is used to grow plants. Different types of plants grow in different types of soil.
2. Soil is the home of many small animals. Earthworm, beetles, ants and snails are some animals that live in soil.

Earthworm

Snail

Ants

Did you know?

Earthworm is called a 'farmer's friend' because they turn and loosen the soil, thus increasing the air and water content in the soil. Moreover, 'worm casts' are very rich in minerals and good for plants.

Do yourself

A. Write the names of the things that soil contains.

Soil

- ____________
- ____________
- Minerals
- ____________

B. Tick (✓) the correct answer.

1. Soil is formed by the action of

   a. Sun and wind ☐

   b. Wind and rain ☐

   c. Sun, wind and rain ☐

2. Time taken to form the soil is

   a. Five years ☐

   b. Million years ☐

   c. Ten years ☐

3. Dead parts of plants and animals in soil are called

   a. Humus ☐

   b. Sand ☐

   c. Pebble ☐

4. Soil provides water and minerals for the growth of

   a. Plants ☐

   b. Farmers ☐

   c. Animals ☐

5. The best soil for plants is

   a. Clay ☐

   b. Sand ☐

   c. Loam ☐

C. Answer the following.

1. What is soil?
2. How is soil formed?
3. What does soil contain?
4. What does the farmer add in the soil to make it more fertile?
5. How is soil useful to us?

D. Unjumble the given words with the help of the given clues.

1. Soil used for making pots

   LAYC ____________________

2. Soil used by farmers to grow plants

   OLMAY ____________________

3. This makes soil rich and fertile

   UHUMS ____________________

4. Soil is formed by breaking this down

   OCRSK ____________________

5. Soil contain it

   OMSIUTER ____________________

E. You have read the lesson. Let's see how much you rembember. Write five to six sentences telling how soil was formed many, many year ago.

Think and tell

- Rajni is playing with soil. She takes some soil in a glass jar and pours water into it. At once she sees bubbles coming out from the soil. Can you tell the reason why?
- Now Rajni has kept aside the jar having soil and water for sometime and is amazed to see that some layers are formed in the jar. Can you guess the types of layers formed? Draw diagram to explain it.

Activity time

- You must be having a clay room in your school. Try these activities there. To make pots with clay. Make various shapes using clay.
- Collects in small plastic packets different samples of soils. Collect at least three samples if not more

4 Solid, Liquid and Gas

You all have seen water in its different forms. When water is kept in a freezer, it forms ice. Ice is the solid form of water. When water is boiled, it changes to steam. Steam is the gaseous form of water. But water is mostly found in a liquid state.

Like water, many other things exist in three forms. These forms are called **states of matter**. The three states are— solid, liquid and gas.

Solids

Things like stone, paper, pen and eraser are solids. Solids have a definite shape and volume. They do not change their shape when moved from one container to another.

Liquids

Substances like water, juices, milk and oil are liquids. Liquids have fixed volume but do not have any definite shape. They take the shape of the containers in which they are kept. Liquid flow easily.

Gases

A gas has no particular shape or size or volume. Like liquids, gases can also flow. Water changes to water vapour on heating. It is a gas. Air is also a type of gas. Actually air is a mixture of many gases. Oxygen is one of the gases which air contains. Oxygen is the gas that we breathe in and carbon dioxide is the gas that we breathe out.

All three states of matter solid, liquid and gas can change from one state to another.

Differences between solids, liquids and gases

Solids	**Liquids**	**Gases**
Solids have a fixed shape.	Liquids do not have fixed shapes. They take the shape of the containers.	Gases do not have fixed shapes.
Solids do not flow easily.	Liquids can flow.	Gases can flow easily.
Solids have definite volumes.	Liquids have fixed volume also.	Gases have no definite volume.

Do yourself

A. Tick (✓) the correct answer.

1. The state in which things have a definite shape

   a. Solid ☐

   b. Liquid ☐

   c. Gas ☐

2. Gaseous form of water is known as

   a. Ice ☐

   b. Water vapour ☐

   c. Water ☐

3. Air is in the form of

   a. Gas ☐

   b. Liquid ☐

   c. Solid ☐

4. Milk is in the form of

   a. Gas ☐

   b. Liquid ☐

   c. Solid ☐

B. Match the items to the correct state.

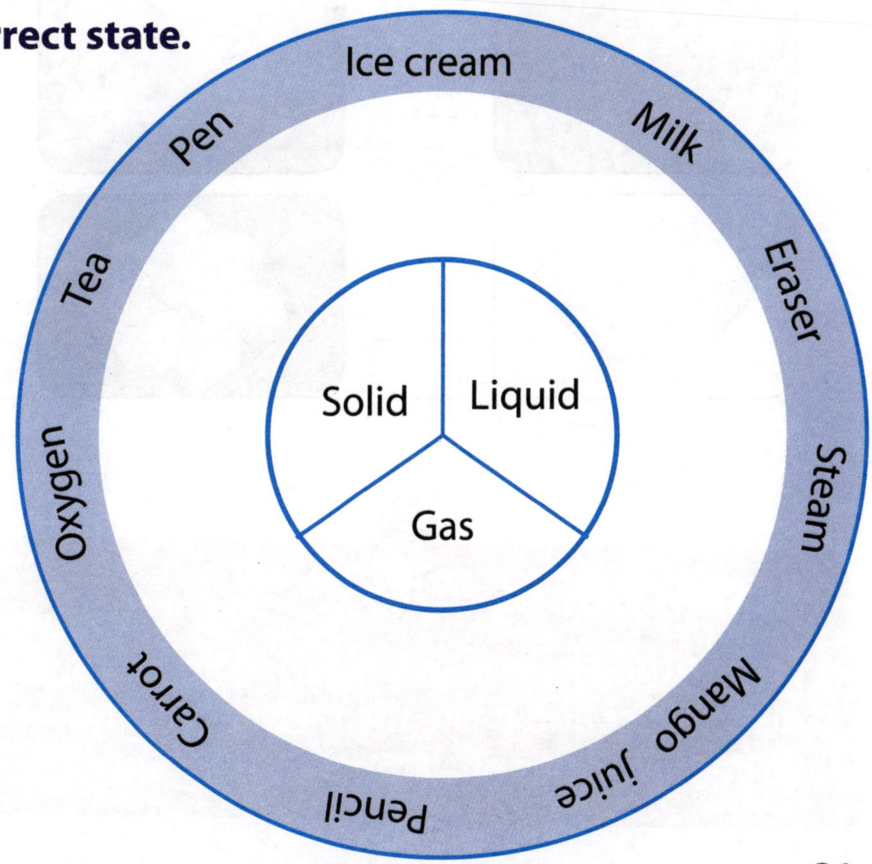

C. Answer the following questions.

1. Give two differences between solids and liquids.
2. Give two examples for each— solids, liquids and gases.
3. Majid puts some ice cubes in the juice that he was drinking. After some time they disappeared. Can you explain why?
4. Write down any two properties of gases.

D. Pinki's mother is preparing a delicious cake. She needs the following things for preparation. Write whether the materials are solid, liquid or gas by writing S, L and G respectively.

Activity time

Collect the pictures of solids and liquids and paste it in your scrapbook. Also collect and paste the pictures of a few things into which gas is filled. Write the names of all the things.

5 Living and Non-living Things

The world is full of amazing things. We see many things around us. We see people, plants animals, birds, cars, , buildings and many more things.

Human beings, animals and plants are **living things**. Living things have life. **Non-living things** have no life. Mountains, rivers, clouds, cars, trains and buildings are non-living things.

Look at the pictures given below and say which are living and which are non-living things in the space given.

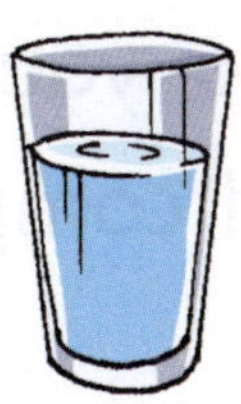

Living things	Non-living things
______________________	______________________
______________________	______________________
______________________	______________________
______________________	______________________
______________________	______________________

There are many features which make living things different from non-living things. Let us learn about them.

Living things grow

A human baby grows into an adult. A puppy grows into a dog. A kitten grows into a cat. A seed grows into a big plant. Living things grow in size.

Can a toy car grow into a big car? Can a doll grow like you? Can a computer grow in size? No, they cannot. Toy car, doll, computer are all non-living things. Non-livings things do not grow.

Toy Engine

Toy Car

Doll

Computer

Living things move

Living things move on their own. Human beings and animals move with the help of their legs. Birds and insects fly and fishes swim. All these move because they have life.

Plants do not move from one place to another. But some parts of the plant show movement in a special way. A sunflower always turns its face towards the sun. The leaves of 'touch me not' plant closes when touched.

Touch me not

Did you know?

The leaves of lotus and portulea plants open out in the morning and close at night.

Look at the table in the picture. Books are lying on the table. Can these books move on their own? Can this table move itself? No, it cannot. Books and tables are non-living things. Non-living things cannot move on their own.

Living things need food

Living things need food to stay alive. Food helps us to grow. It gives us energy to work and play.

Animals also need food. They get their food from plants and other animals.

Plants also need food to grow. They make their own food with the help of air, water and sunlight.

Do your toys need food? No, toys, tables, chairs, books, bags, rocks, and computers are non-living things. Non- living things do not need food.

Living things breathe

All living things breathe. We need air to breathe. We breathe through our nose. Like us, animals also breathe in air. Most of the animals breathe through their nose. Fishes have gills to breathe. Some animals breathe through air holes in their body like cockroaches, mosquitoes and butterflies.

Plants also breathe through tiny holes in their leaves. These are called **stomata**.

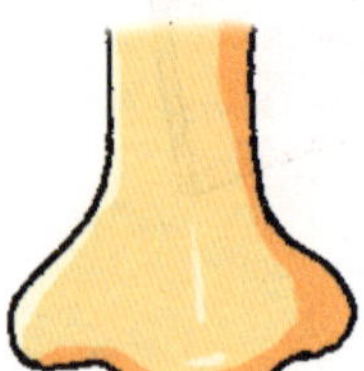

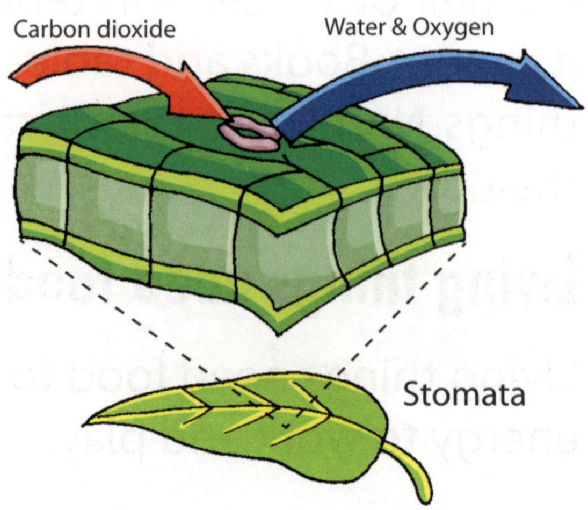

Does your doll breathe like you? It doesn't as non-living things do not breathe.

Living things feel

You feel happy when you get a gift and sometimes you feel pain or become angry or even cry. Yes, we all do so because we can feel. Animals can also feel. Cats purr when you stroke it. Plants can also feel. 'Touch me not' plant feels a touch. Plants can also feel light and so grows towards it. A plant grows much faster if you stroke it lovingly everyday! So you see that all living things feel.

Toys, cars, book, pencil are non-living things. Non living things do not feel.

Living things reproduce

Giving birth to young ones is called **reproduction**. All living things reproduce. Animals reproduce by either laying eggs or giving birth to young ones. Birds and fishes lay eggs from which babies hatch. Most new plants grow from seeds.

Can a book reproduce another book? Can your doll give birth to a baby doll? No. This is because books and dolls are non-living things and non-living things do not reproduce.

Non-living things can further be divided into natural things and man-made things.

Hens with its chicks

Mother with her baby

Bird with eggs

Cow with its calf

Natural things

Things like animals, plants, birds, rocks, rivers, clouds, the sun, the moon and the stars are not made by man. Nature has given these things to us. They are called **natural things**. Natural things maybe living or non-living

Man-made things

Things like tables, chairs, books, cars, buses, roads, buildings, houses are made by man. They are called **man-made** things. Man-made things are non-living things.

Do yourself

A. Encircle the odd one.

1.	Dog	Cat	Cow	Pen
2.	Cub	Calf	Kitten	Dog
3.	Book	Pencil	Flower	Eraser
4.	Stars	Moon	Bridge	River.

B. Tick (✓) the correct answer.

1. Living things
   a. Can grow ☐
   b. Cannot feel ☐
   c. Cannot breathe ☐

2. This is a man-made thing
   a. Cloud ☐
   b. Building ☐
   c. Hill ☐
3. This is a non-living thing
   a. Rose plant ☐
   b. Teddy bear ☐
   c. Lamb ☐
4. This is a natural thing
   a. Sun ☐
   b. Bulb ☐
   c. Car ☐

C. Answer the following.

1. Why cannot a plant move from place to place?
2. Write any four features of living things.
3. Name any two things which are non-living but natural.
4. What are man-made things? Give any two examples.
5. Name any two organs that various animals use to breathe.
6. What is reproduction?

D. Match the following

A	B
Pigeon	Gills
Plant	Kitten
Cat	Egg
Fish	Seed

E. Find the answers of following in the given word grid.

a. The young one of this animal is called a 'kid'

b. The pores on the leaf through which the plant breathes

c. Birds lay eggs in it

d. A baby cat

e. Frozen water

f. Living things breathe in this

g. Plant grows from it

I	S	H	G	L	W	Q	G	L
C	F	S	F	J	K	I	D	D
E	H	J	D	G	X	A	A	R
Q	D	N	W	C	M	P	T	Y
S	T	O	M	A	T	A	C	T
D	B	N	O	G	T	Y	L	N
V	D	L	K	P	V	X	B	K
N	E	S	T	K	E	R	A	I
H	F	G	K	A	I	R	Q	T
N	L	P	R	X	Z	B	D	T
W	E	N	L	Y	V	I	G	E
V	S	C	K	J	Q	N	M	N
B	S	S	E	E	D	K	G	W

F. Write the name of five living and five non-living things from your surroundings. Write whether the non-living things are manmade of natural.

Living things	**Non-living things** (Man-made or natural)

G. **Look at the picture carefully. Write (L) for living and (N) for non-living things on the picture.**

Activity time

Paste the pictures five non-living things in your scrapbook that can move.

6 Our Body

You are familiar with the various parts of our body— **internal** and **external**. Eyes, nose, ears, hand, legs are some of the external parts of the body and brain, stomach, lungs, heart are some of the internal parts.

Have you ever felt that some hard parts exist inside your body? Those are the bones of your body. Along with the hard parts there are soft parts also under our skin. Those are our muscles.

Bones

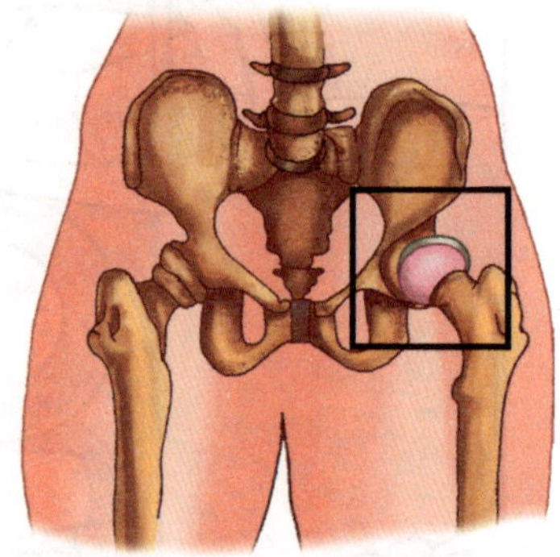

Hip Joint

The bones give shape and support to our body. Bones are hard and stiff. They protect the soft parts of our body which are lying inside.

There are 206 bones in our body. Some bones are big while others are small.

Bone joints

Bone joint is a place where two or more bones are joined together. We can bend the parts of our body because of the joints.

The Skeleton

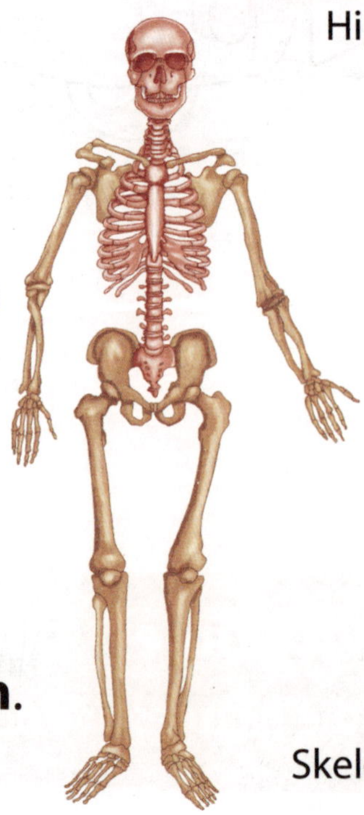

Skeleton

The bones of our body form a frame work. This framework of bones is called the **skeleton**. It gives shape and support to our body.

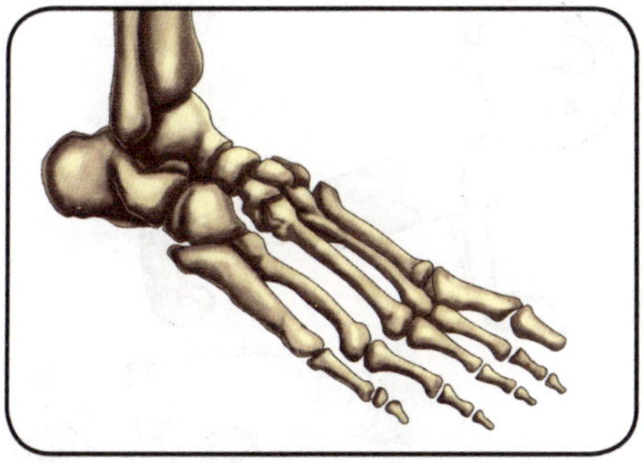
Joints in the foot

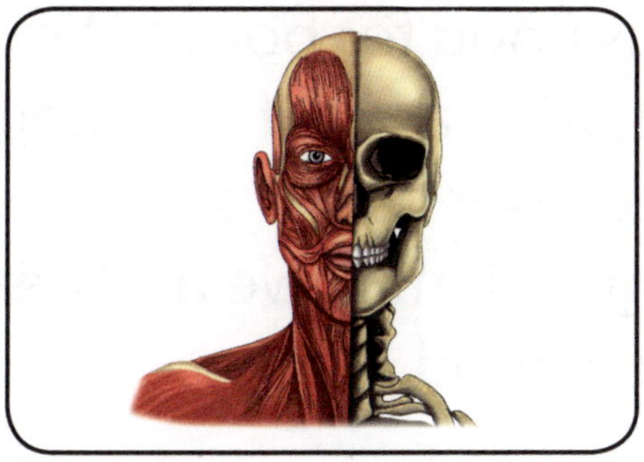
Bones and Muscles

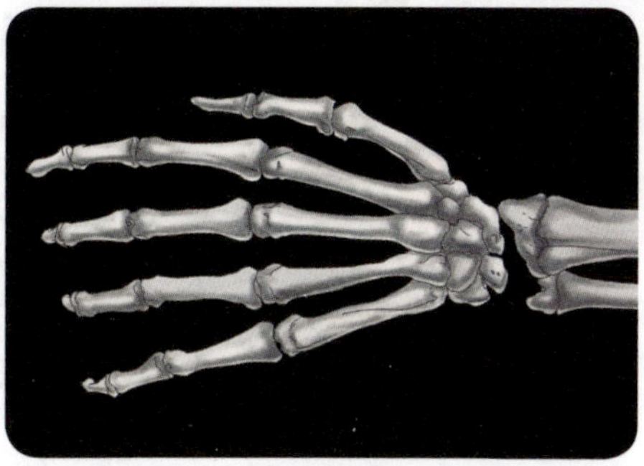
Finger and Wrist Joints

Muscles

The soft portion under our skin are the muscles. Muscles cover the bones and help in the movement of the bones.

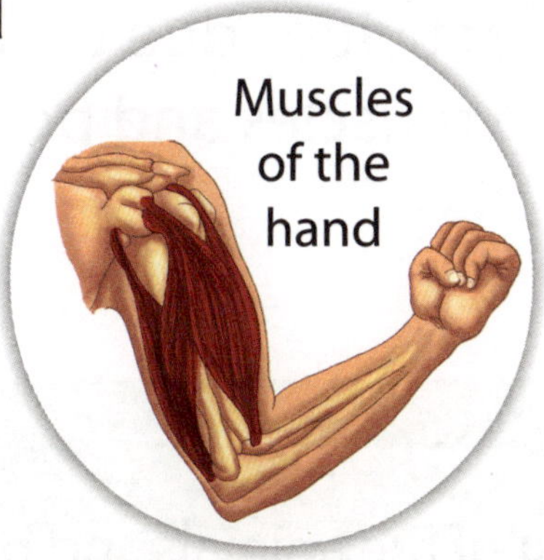
Muscles of the hand

Muscles help us to open our eyes, to smile, to frown, to swallow our food and do much more.

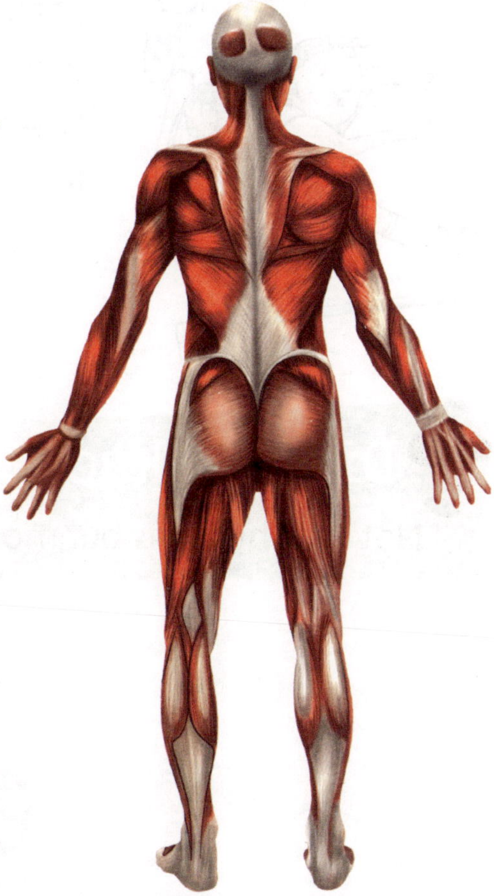
Muscles of the body

Exercise and food

Bones and muscles of our body must be strong. To have strong bones and muscles we need to do exercise and eat healthy food everyday.

Healthy Food

Milk

Milk is good for bones. We must drink a lot of milk daily to keep our bones strong. Along with milk we must eat healthy food.

Exercise makes our muscles strong. We must do it daily. Strong muscles help us to work and play without being tired. Sports persons can do lot of activities due to their strong muscles and bones.

Did you know?

Not only humans but most of the animals and birds also have bones and muscles

Do yourself

A. Give one word for the following.

1. Hard and stiff part of our body
2. Two or more bones are joined together at the
3. Bones are covered with
4. The framework of bones is called a
5. Exercise makes it strong

B. Abhi and Shrey are discussing the facts about bones and muscles. They are wrong in some places. Find it and write the correct word in the space given.

Shrey: Abhi, do you know that muscles give shape to our bodies?

___

Abhi: Yes. And, we must drink lot of water to make our bones strong, right?

___

Shrey: Yes I think so. The framework of muscles is called the skeleton, isn't it?

___

Abhi: Shrey, do you know we have 600 bones in our body. Bones protect the soft inner parts of our bodies.

___

Shrey: Yes I know. And the bones are covered with skin, isn't it?

___

C. Answer the following.

1. How are bones useful to us?
2. What is a bone joint? How are joints useful to us?
3. How do muscles help our body?
4. What do you understand by skeleton?
5. How can we make our bones and muscles strong?

D. Complete the following crossword puzzles with the help of the clues.

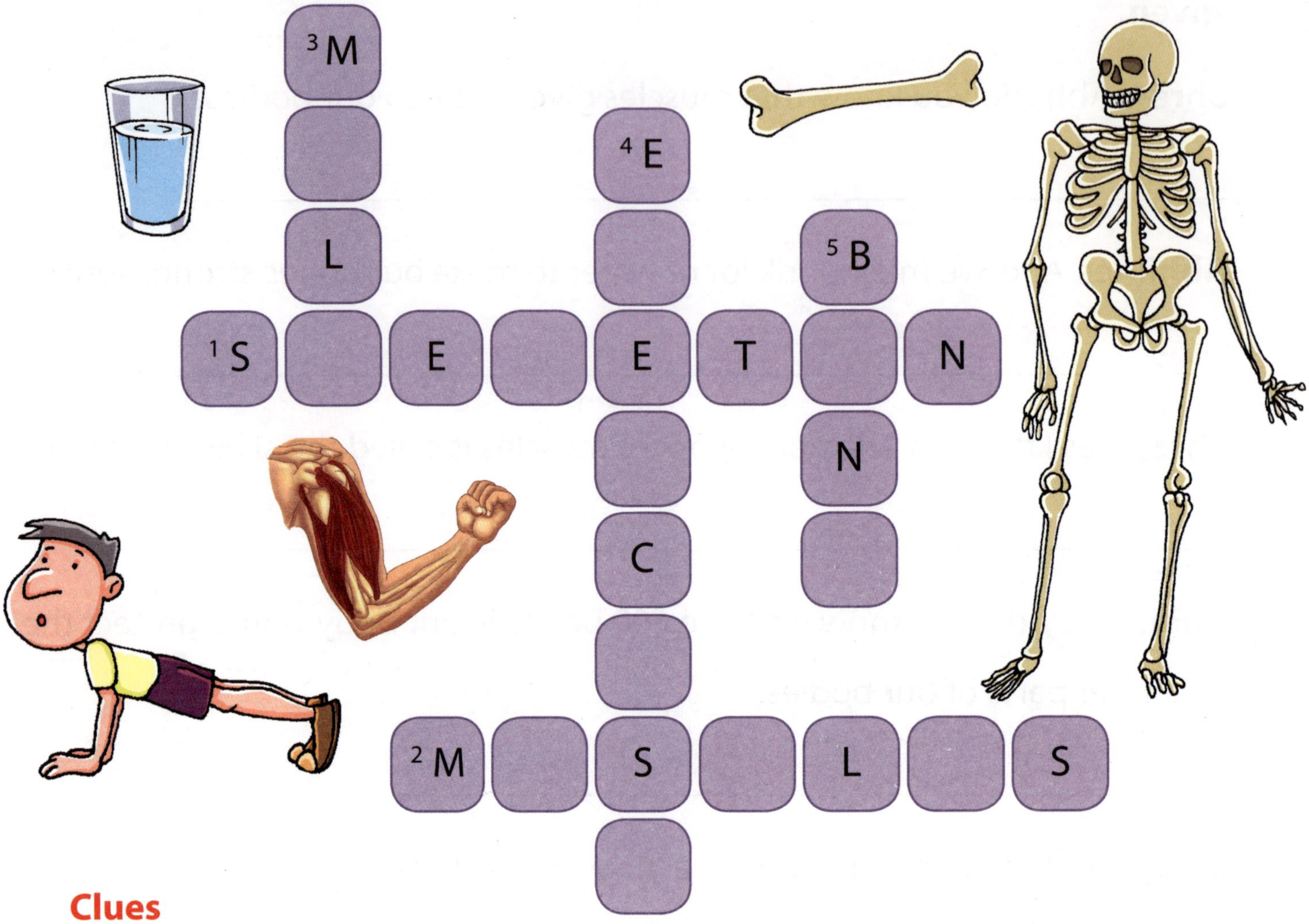

Clues

Across

1. The bony framework of our body
2. The soft portion of our body under our skin

Downward

3. The white drink that makes our bones strong
4. We should do it regularly to keep fit
5. The hard and stiff part of our body whose name starts with B

E. **All the friends of Abhi are exercising in the park. Abhi wants to join them. Help him find the way to his friends.**

F. Time to memorize

Give below is the picture of the human brain. The parts are clearly marked and labelled. Learn the names of its parts.

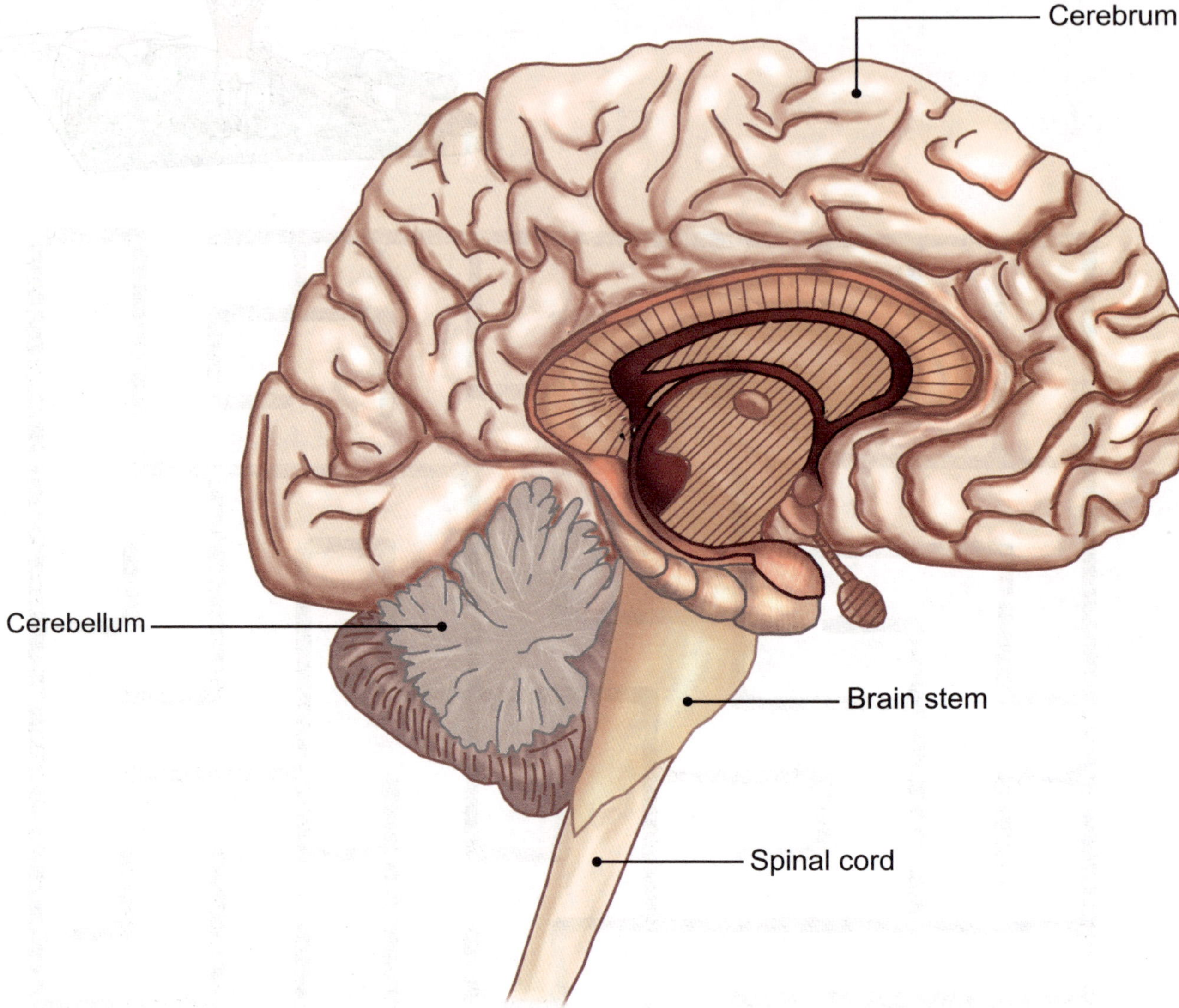

Activity time

1. Collect the pictures of exercises and yoga that make our muscles strong. Paste them in your scrapbook.
2. Visit National Historical Museum with teachers or elders and see the skeleton of ancient animals. Make a list of the other things you see there.

7 Plants and Animals

Plants and animals are both living things. Yet they are different from each other in many ways. Let us see how they differ from each other.

Movement

Animals can move from one place to another. They move in search of food. A lion roams about in a jungle. A monkey jumps from one tree to another. A cat runs after a rat. Birds fly from one place to another.

On the other hand plants are fixed to the ground. They do not move in search of food. They make their own food.

Food habits

Animals cannot make their own food. Animals eat plants or other animals. Animals like cows, buffaloes and horses eat plants only. Animals like lions and tigers eat the flesh of other animals.

Like animals, plants also need food. Green plants make their own food with the help of air, water and sunlight. Only non-green plants like mushrooms, moulds get their food from dead and decaying matter.

Mushroom

Did you know?

Plants are green due to the presence of chlorophyll in them. It helps them in making food.

Pitcher Plant

Venus Fly Trap

Certain plants trap insects for food like the Pitcher plant or the Venus flytrap!

Breathing

All animals need air to breathe. Animals breathe through their lungs, gills and air holes. Animals like cows, horses, tigers, giraffes and whales breathe through their lungs. Fishes have gills to breathe in water. Insects like butterflies, cockroaches and flies have holes on their bodies. They breathe through these holes.

Plants also breathe. They do not have lungs or gills. Leaves of plants have tiny pores on them. These pores are called **stomata**. Plants breathe through their stomata. (singular stoma)

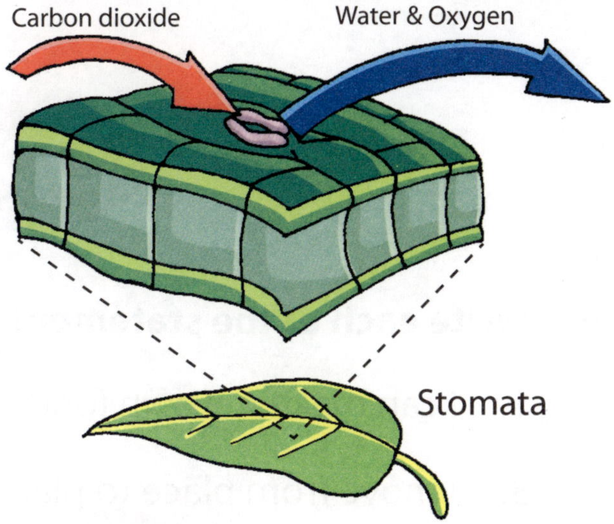

Sense organs

Animals have sense organs like the skin, eyes, nose, ears and tongue. These organs help them to know the world around them.

Plants do not have sense organs. But they show response to the changes. 'Touch me not plant' closes its leaves when we touch it.

Reproduction

Animals give birth to their young ones. Some animals like birds, snakes and frogs lay eggs. Some animals like cats, dogs and cows give birth to their young ones like themselves.

Plants cannot give birth to young ones or lay eggs. Most plants reproduce from seeds. Seeds give rise to new plants. Some new plants grow from certain parts of some plants like the stem, root or leaves.

Both animals and plants are wonderful creatures. They add to the beauty of our world. We should care for them and protect them.

Do Yourself

A. Write each of the statements with the correct picture.

1. I can make my own food
2. I have gills to breathe
3. I move from place to place.

____

____

____

B. Tick (✓) the correct answer.

1. Green plants need these to make their food

   a. Air, water and sunlight ☐

   b. Air and water ☐

   c. Water and sunlight ☐

2. Animals that breathe through holes in their bodies

   a. Cows and tigers ☐

   b. Fish and flies ☐

   c. Flies and cockroaches ☐

3. Most plants breathe through tiny pores on their

   a. Flowers ☐

   b. Leaves ☐

   c. Roots ☐

4. Animals that reproduce by laying eggs

   a. Birds and snakes ☐

   b. Cats and dogs ☐

   c. Frogs and dogs ☐

C. Answer the questions given below.

1. Why do animals move from place to place?
2. How do green plants make their food?
3. How do plants breathe?
4. Write the different ways by which the living things breathe.
5. How do plants reproduce?

D. Unscramble the letters to get the answer.

1. Plants are ____________ (IXFDE) to the ground.
2. Tigers and lions eat the ____________ (LEHFS) of other animals.

3. ____________ (MSURHMOOS) get their food from dead and decaying matter.

4. Fishes breathe through ____________ (ILGLS).

5. We should ____________ (ROPTETC) both animals and plants.

Activity time

- Plants feel the changes around them. Take a small potted plant. Place it near a window through which light can come in. What do you notice after a few days? Discuss with you teacher.
- Magic with fingers
  Dip your thumb in a paint bottle and make the following figures with it.

- Plant a sapling on your birthday. Water it and watch it grow every day. Take a note of its growth until your next birthday comes.

8 Parts of a Plant

A plant has different parts. Each part of plant has a special function. Let us read about these parts.

Root and shoot

A plant body has mainly two parts—the **root** and the **shoot**. The part of a plant that grows below the ground is called the **root**. The part of a plant that grows above the ground is called the **shoot**.

The root

There are two types of roots—**tap root** and **fibrous root**.

Taproot

It is the main root that grows from the end of the stem in the soil. Many smaller roots grow from this root. Plants like balsam, pea, bean, mustard, carrot, neem, mango and peepal have taproot.

Tap Root

Fibrous root

When a number of roots grow from the end of the stem, it is called **fibrous root**. Plants like grass, wheat, rice, onion, maize have fibrous roots.

Fibrous Root

Functions of roots

Roots have many functions.

1. Roots fix plants in the soil.
2. Roots absorb water and minerals from the soil and send them to the different parts of a plant.
3. The roots of some plants store food in them. These roots are edible vegetables like carrot, radish, turnip and beet root.

Turnip

Carrot

Radish

Beetroot

Shoot

The shoot of a plant has the stem, branches, leaves, buds, flowers and fruits.

Stem

The stem is the main part of the shoot. The hard and woody stem is called the **trunk**. Trees like banyan, neem and mango have strong and woody stems. Some plants have weak and woody stem like the rose.

Some plants like money plant have soft, green and weak stems. It needs support to stay upright.

Money Plant

Tree

Functions of the stem

The main functions of the stem are:

1. It holds the plant upright and supports the leaves and flowers.
2. It carries water and mineral salts from the roots to the leaves.
3. It carries food made by leaves to all parts of the plant.
4. It stores the food in some plants like sugarcane, onion, potato and ginger. We eat the stems of these plants.
5. Cactus, the desert plant stores water in its stem.

Sugar Cane

Potato

Onion

Ginger

Leaves

Leaf is the most important part of a plant. Most plants have green leaves and leaves are of different sizes and shapes.

The flat and broad part of a leaf is called the **leaf blade** or **lamina**. The tip of the leaf is called the **leaf apex**. In the middle of the leaf runs the **main vein** and its branches are called the **side veins**. These veins carry water to the leaf. The underside of the leaf has tiny pores called **stomata**. Plants breathe air through these stomata.

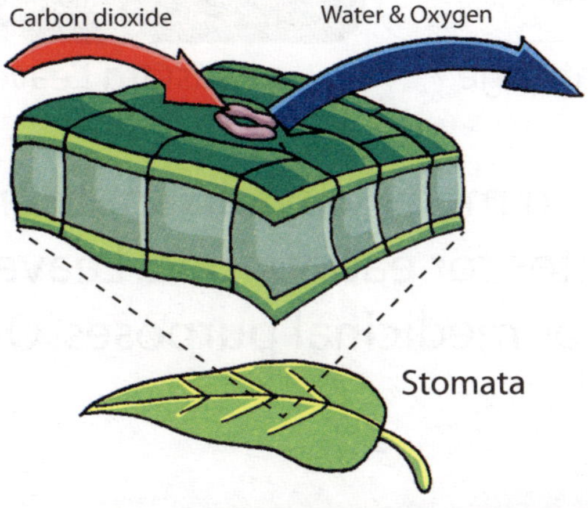

Different types of leaves

Did you know?

Potato, ginger and onion are underground stems.

Functions of leaves

Leaf is an important part of the plant. Let's study the various functions of leaves.

1. A leaf is called the **food factory** or kitchen of the plant. A green leaf makes food for the plant with the help of air, water and sunlight. This process is called **photosynthesis**.
2. Leaves give out oxygen while making food. This happens during the day. Oxygen is very important for life. Human beings and animals breathe in oxygen to stay alive.
3. Leaves breathe in oxygen and breathe out carbon dioxide at night.
4. Leaves of some plants such as cabbage, spinach, mustard, lettuce and fenugreek (methi), store food in them. These are green vegetables and are good for health. Leaves of mint, corianders and curry plant are used for garnishing and flavouring the food.

Spinach

Lettuce

Cabbage

Mustard Leaves

Leaves have become a part of our daily life in many ways. In southern part of India, banana leaves are used as plates for eating food. Leaves of some plants like Tulsi and Neem are used for medicinal purposes. Often,

Corriander Leaves

Curry Leaves

Mint Leaves

we see pictures of leaves at differnt places like curtains, bed covers, sarees and dress material.

Bed Spread

Flower

The flower is the most beautiful part of a plant. Most plants bear flowers. Most of the flowers change into fruits.

Bougainvillea

Rose

Marigold

Functions of flowers

1. Most flowers produce fruits.
2. Flowers attract insects which help in the reproduction.
3. Flowers help the plants look beautiful and attractive.

Fruits and seeds

Fruits are formed from flowers. Fruits have seeds inside them. Some fruits have one seed. Some have a few seeds while others have many.

Papaya

Mango

Apple

A mango has one seed, an orange or an apple have a few seeds. A papaya has many seeds.

Most plants grow from seeds

Seeds are protected inside the fruit. Each seed has a baby plant inside it. When the seed gets enough air, water and warmth, the baby plant starts growing. This process is called **germination**. It grows into a young plant and keeps on growing till it becomes a fully grown plant.

Did you know?

Banana seeds do not grow into new plants.

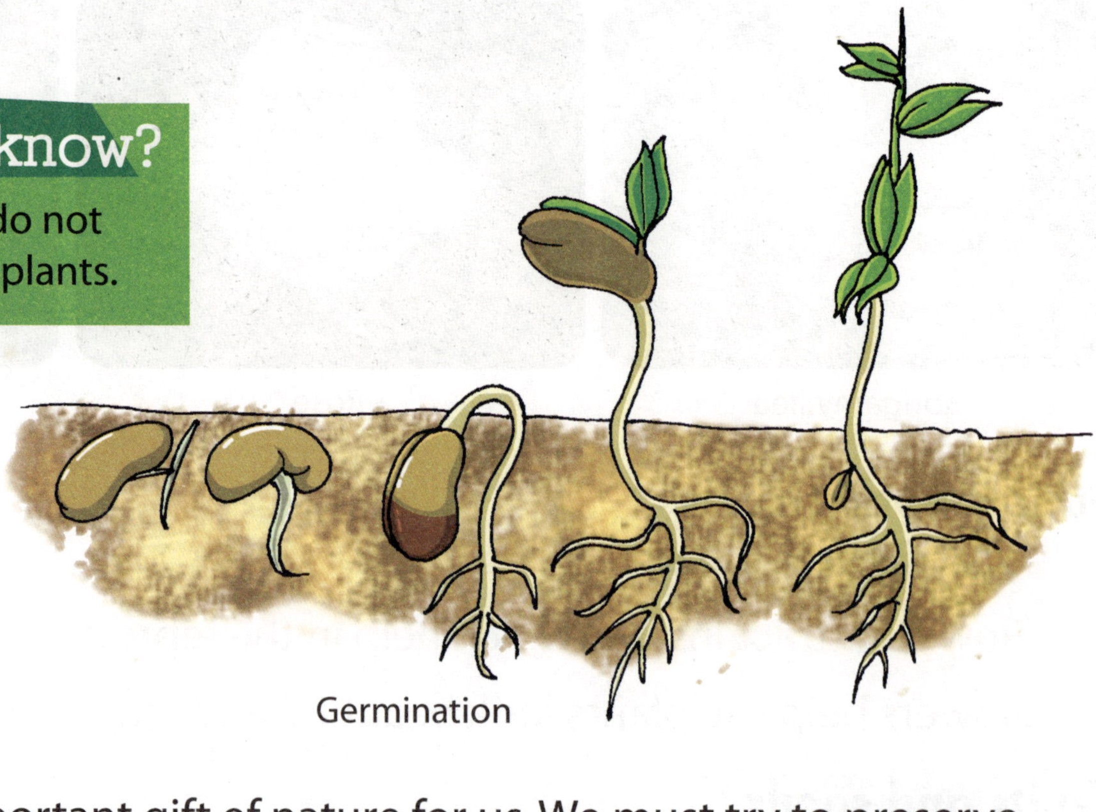

Germination

Plants are an important gift of nature for us. We must try to preserve plants and grow as many as we can.

Do Yourself

A. Tick (✓) the correct answer.

1. Potato is a

   a. Stem ☐

   b. Leaf ☐

   c. Root ☐

2. The leaf of a plant is called its

   a. Bedroom ☐

   b. Kitchen ☐

   c. Storeroom ☐

3. Plants breathe in air through their

   a. Leaf ☐

   b. Stem ☐

   c. Roots ☐

4. The process by which plants prepare their food is called

   a. Germination ☐

   b. Reproduction ☐

   c. Photosynthesis ☐

B. A wheel with different parts of plant is given here. Colour the part of the wheel according to the instruction given.

Brown: fixes the plant in the soil

Blue: grows into new plant

Green: makes food for the plant

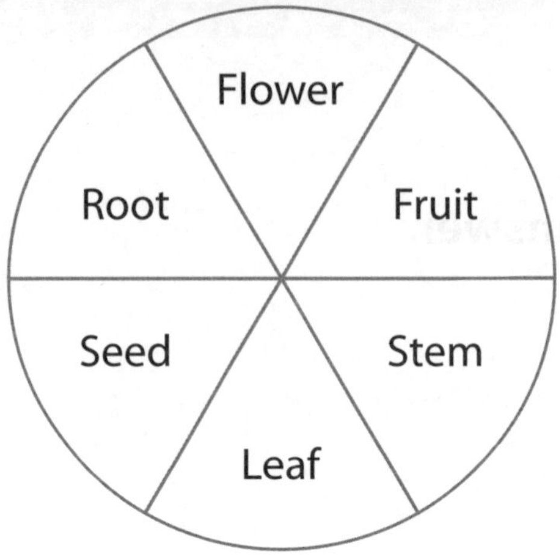

Red: changes into fruit

Pink: has seed inside it

Yellow: holds the plant upright

C. Answer the following questions.

1. Write any two functions of the root.
2. Write any two functions of the stem.
3. Why is a leaf called the kitchen of the plant?
4. What is the purpose of stomata?
5. What does a seed need to grow into a plant?

D. Complete the following pictures by adding the names of other vegetables.

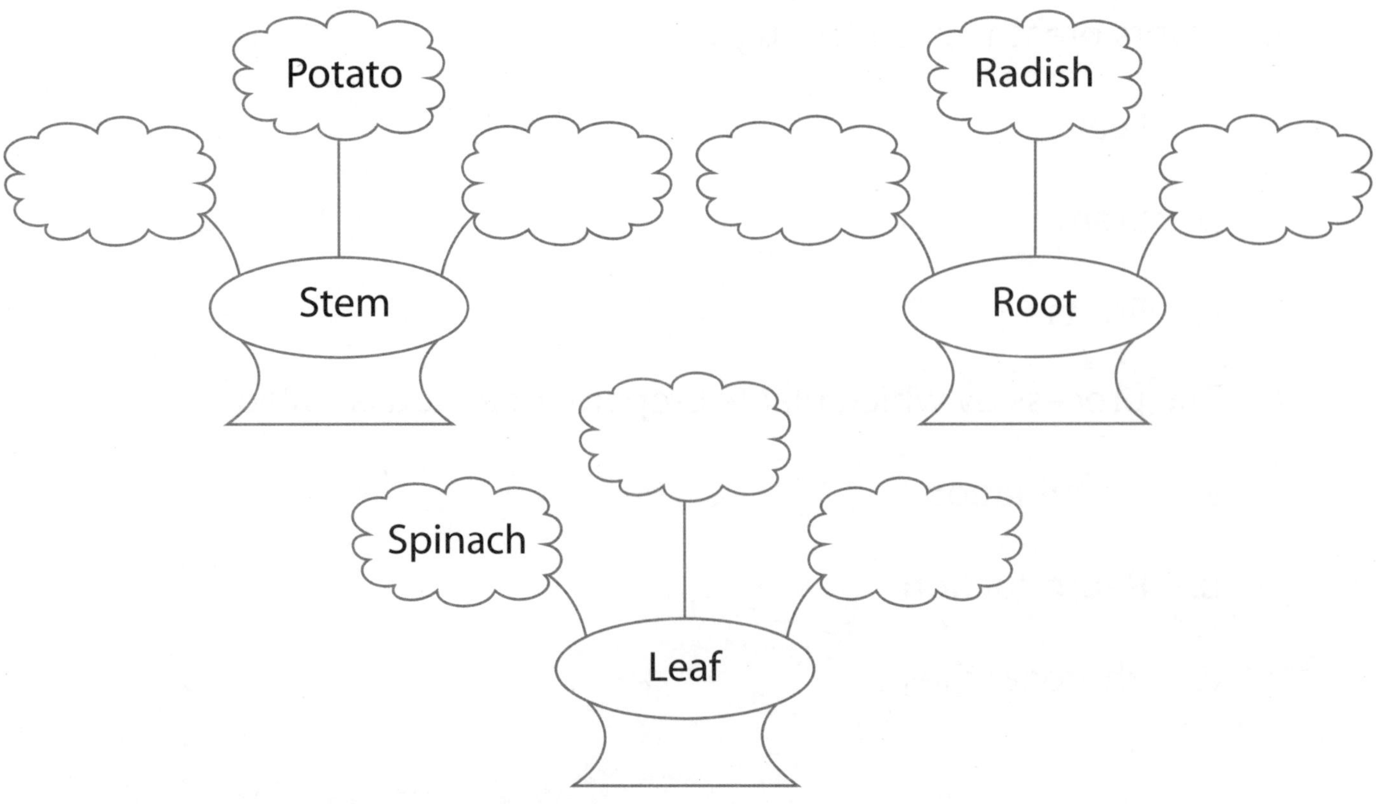

E. Here is a word grid given to you. Read the clues and find the answer in the word grid.

1. It has tap root and the name starts with m.
2. It is a leafy vegetable that we eat
3. Most flowers grow into these
4. It grows below the ground
5. It is the beautiful part of the plant

N	C	A	B	B	A	G	E	S	R
L	X	F	R	B	H	R	K	D	O
A	B	Q	O	L	A	S	F	F	O
Q	D	F	O	W	Q	Q	J	V	T
M	U	S	T	A	R	D	Q	H	T
G	P	S	F	D	D	P	W	I	Y
H	H	F	L	O	W	E	R	K	U
J	A	G	D	X	K	F	S	R	J
L	S	E	A	Z	L	V	X	W	L
F	R	U	I	T	T	G	N	E	K

Activity time

- Collect different types of flowers. Do not pluck them. Pick any fallen ones. Keep the flowers in a book for a few days. The flowers will become dry. Now paste them in your scrapbook. Write the name of each flower.
- Take a leaf from your garden. Turn it over on a table and place a blank paper on it. Now take a colour pencil or a pencil and start shading on it. After a while, you will see that the impression of the leaf becomes clearly visible on the blank paper.

- Take a white flower (chrysanthemum) and chop its stem in a slanting manner. Now take some coloured water in a glass and dip the flower into the coloured water. The colour of the flower will change into the colour of the water! This is because the stem carries the water to the flower.

- Collect different types of seeds. Paste them in your scrapbook.
- Collect dry leaves from your garden. Let's make pictures of animals using these dry leaves.

9 Amazing Birds

Birds are living things that can fly in the air. There are many different kinds of birds of different sizes and colours. There are some special features that make birds unique.

Special features of their body

1. A bird has a boat shaped body. It helps it to cut through the air.
2. It has wings which helps it to fly.
3. Feathers are attached to the wings. A bird has two types of feathers— **down feathers** and **flight feathers**. Down feathers are those that cover the body. They are small and fluffy. They help the bird to keep warm. Flight feathers are those which are attached to the wings. They are flat and long. They help the birds to fly.

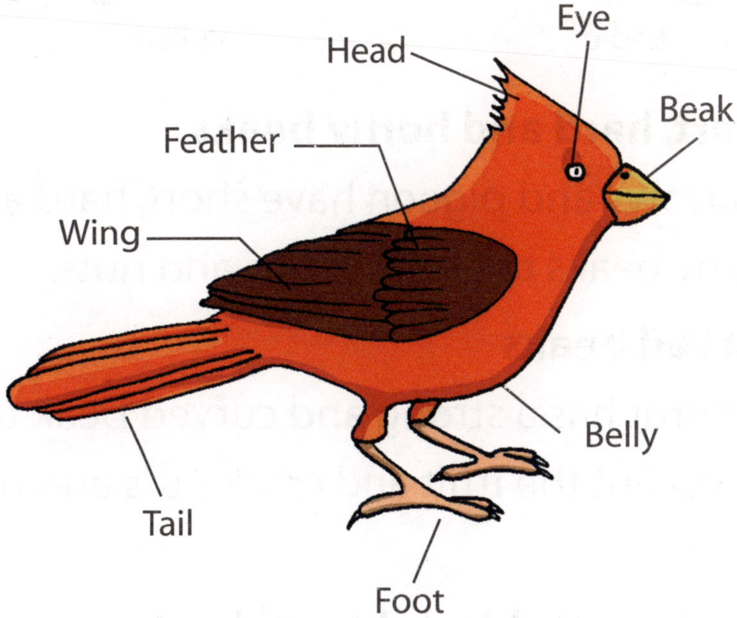

Parts of a Bird

4. The tail of a bird acts like a rudder of a boat. It helps the bird to change direction while flying.

5. Birds have very light body because of their hollow bones.
6. They have beaks and claws to catch, hold and eat their food. They have no teeth.

Beaks of birds

Different birds have different kinds of beaks.

Strong sharp and hooked beaks

Eagles, vultures, kites and owls have strong sharp and hooked beaks to tear flesh. They are called **birds of prey**.

Eagle

Vulture

Short, hard and horny beaks

Sparrows and pigeon have short, hard and horny beaks to crush grains and nuts.

Sparrow

Pigeon

Curved beaks

A parrot has a strong and curved beak to scoop out the fruit and crack nuts and hard fruits.

Parrot

Strong and chisel shaped beaks

A woodpecker has strong and chisel-shaped beak. It helps to tap the bark of trees and take out insects to eat.

Woodpecker

Broad and flat beaks

Ducks, geese and a few cranes have broad and flat beaks with holes on either side. These birds take in muddy water with insects, worms and plants. The muddy water flows out through tiny holes leaving plants and insects inside the beak.

Ducks

Long and pointed beaks

Humming birds and sunbirds have long and pointed beak to poke into flowers and look for nectors.

Humming bird

Long and slender beaks

A hoopoe's beak is long and slender. It helps the bird to pull out insects from holes in the ground or trees.

Hoopoe

Feet and claws of birds

Birds use their claws to catch and eat their food. They also use them to protect themselves from their enemies. They also use their feet and claws to perch on the branches.

Flesh eating birds

Flesh eating birds such as hawks eagles, kites and vultures have strong and sharp claws called **talons**. With the help of talons, they catch live animals like toads, mice and rats.

Eagle's Claw

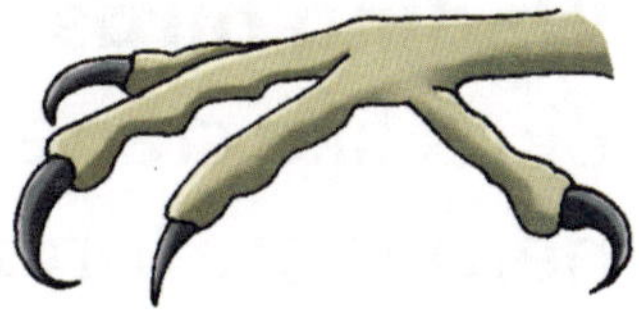

Hawk's Claw

Perching birds

Perching birds like crows, sparrows, pigeons and parrots have three toes in front and one at the back. These help the birds to hold on to a branch. This is called **perching**.

Scratching birds

Birds like hens have sharp claws to dig and scratch the ground.

Climbing birds

Birds like woodpeckers and parakeets have two toes pointing upwards and two toes pointing in the downward direction. These help them to climb up and hold on to trees.

Swimming birds

The birds like ducks, geese and pelicans have webbed feet. They have three toes in front and one toe at the back. The three toes are joined by their skin called a **web**. This helps them to swim.

Wading birds

Birds like cranes, flamingoes and herons are long legged with spread out toes. They can wade through muddy water without getting wet.

Crow's Feet

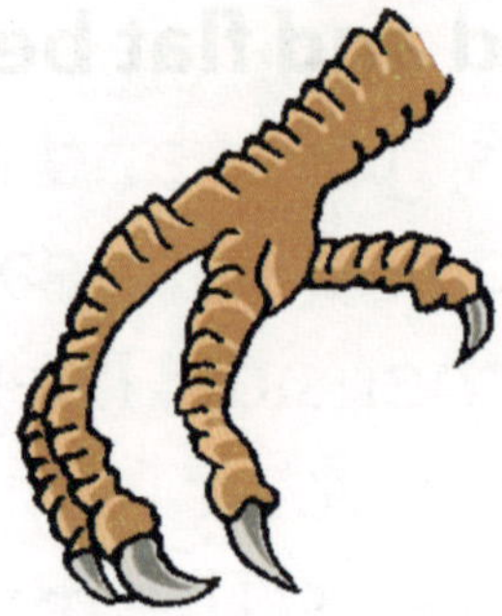

Pigeion's Feet

Hen's Feet

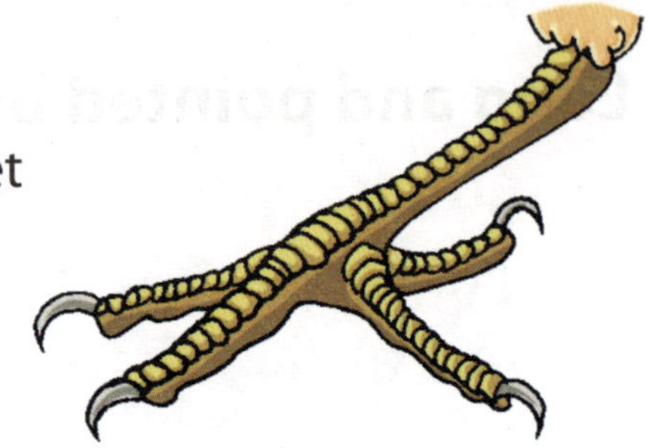

Woodpecker's Feet

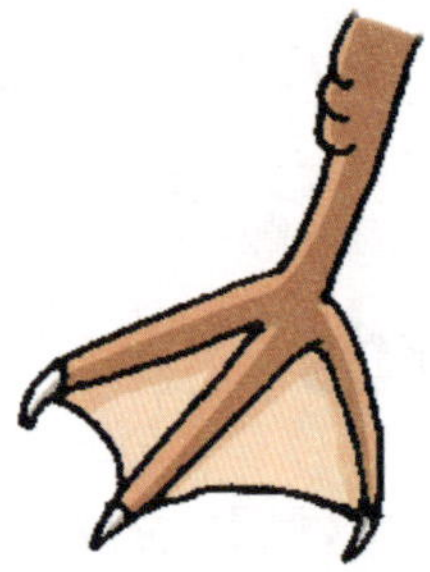

Duck's feet

Goose's Feet

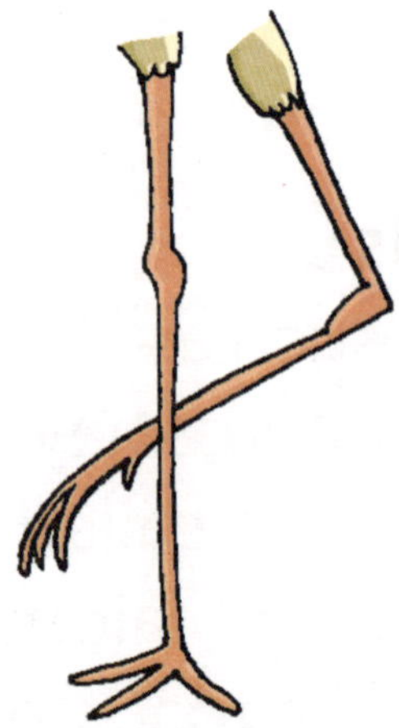

Crane's Feet

Flamingo's Feet

Nests of birds

A bird's home is called a **nest**. Different birds make different types of nest. Birds use leaves, straws, twigs, wool, cotton and thread to build their nest. They choose places which are safe from enemies and bad weather.

A Nest

Tailor Bird's Nest

Weaver Bird's Nest

Birds lay their eggs in the nests. After sometime the eggs hatch and baby birds come out. Birds keep their young ones safe and warm in the nest. Some of these nests are made in a special way.

Different types of birds have different ways of making nests.

The tailor bird's nest

It uses its beak like a needle to sew leaves together to build a nest. It uses materials like thread and wool to sew the leaves. That is why it is called **tailor bird**.

The weaver bird's nest

It uses leaves, grass and twigs to weave a beautiful nest. The nest hangs from the branch of a tree. The bird enters its home through a tunnel like opening at the bottom of nest.

The woodpecker's nest

It uses its beak to peck in the tree trunk to make a hole for a nest.

The penguin's nest

The penguin collects a few pebbles and stones to make their nest on

Woodpecker

Penguin

Siberian Crane

the ground. Some birds like cuckoos lay their eggs in other birds nest, generally in the crows' nest.

Some birds live in cold regions. But when temperature becomes very low, they find it difficult to tolerate. So they fly to warmer areas during the winters. This is known as **migration**. Siberian cranes, painted stork are some birds that migrate to India in winters from different parts of the world. They fly back to their cold homes when summer starts.

Do yourself

A. Name the bird that does the following.

1. Weaves grass in and out to make a nest
2. Its front toes are joined by a skin
3. Collects pebbles and stones to make nest
4. Uses its beak to peck into the tree
5. Sews leaves together to build their nest

B. Match the following

1.  broad beaks with holes

2.  short, hard and horny beak

3.  Help to scoop out the fruit

4.  Help to tear flesh

C. Tick (✓) the correct answer

1. These birds have three toes in front and one at the back to hold the branch.

   a. Sparrows and pigeons

   b. Woodpeckers and parakeets

   c. Ducks and geese

2. This bird has long and slender beak to help in to pull out insects from holes in ground.

   a. Woodpecker

   b. Hoopoes

   c. Humming bird

3. These birds of prey have strong, sharp claws called talons

   a. Vultures and pigeons

   b. Kites

c. Sparrows ☐

4. The body of bird is

a. Boat-shaped ☐

b. Apple-shaped ☐

c. Pin- shaped ☐

5. A bird that makes hole is the tree trunk to make a nest

a. Weaver bird ☐

b. Woodpecker ☐

c. Tailor bird ☐

D. Answer the following.

1. Write any three features of birds.
2. What is the function of strong, sharp and hooked shaped beaks?
3. Which bird has strong chisel-shaped beak? What is the purpose of it?
4. How are the birds like duck and geese able to swim?
5. Why do birds make nest?
6. How is the beak useful to a bird?
7. What is migration?

E. Who am I?

a. My beak is very special; I use it like a needle. By stitching leaves I make my home. I am called the ____________ bird.

b. I am the national bird of India. On my head I have a crest. I have beautiful greenish blue feathers. I am a ____________

c. My beak is red, my feathers are green. I love green chillies. ____________ is my name.

d. My feathers are grey, gutter goo I do all the day. My eyes are red, I have a blue necklace. ____________ is my name.

F. Join the dots and colour the bird you get.

Activity time

- Make a paper bird. The steps are given below with pictures. Follow them and make your bird.

Step 1: Make a centre crease by folding the paper.

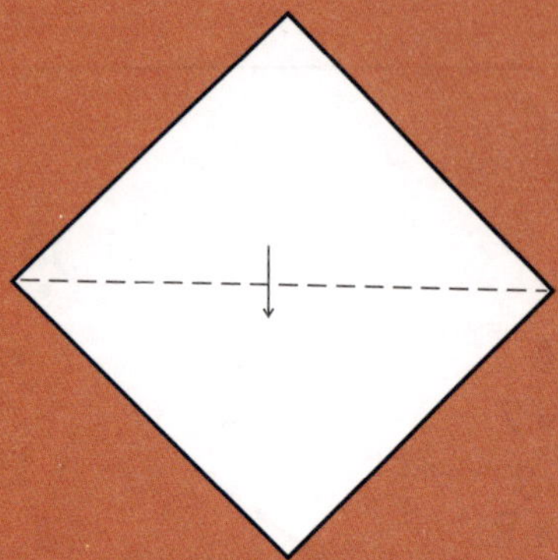

Step 2: Now fold the paper into a triangle. Fold the lower tip backwards along the dotted line.

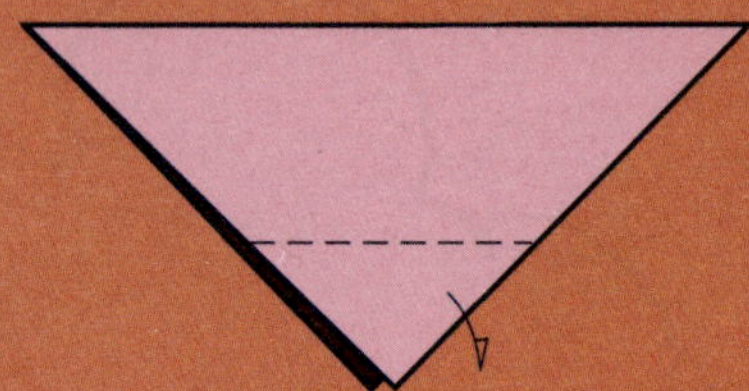

Step 3: Fold the end tip backwards and the front tip towards the front to form the tail and the head.

Step 4: Draw a pair of eyes. Your bird is ready to fly.

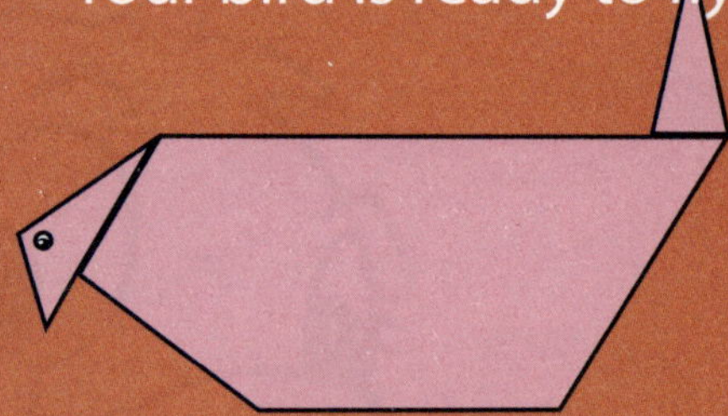

- Collect feathers of birds which you find lying around. Study their shape, size and colours and discuss about it in the class. Make the picture of a bird in your scrapbook and paste the feather on it.
- Divide the class into groups. Each group will make a chart for the given topic and display it in the class.

Group 1: Special features of birds

Group 2: Beaks of birds

Group 3: Feet and claws of birds

Group 4: Nests and birds

10 Measurement

We need to measure many different things in our daily life. A greengrocer weighs vegetables, a tailor measures cloth to make a dresses, a doctor measures body the temperature of his patients, and a goldsmith measures the gold very precisely. We measure various things in our everyday life. In this chapter we will learn how to measure length, weight and capacity.

We have some standard units given by General Conference on Weight and Measures (CGPM) to measure the physical quantities. These standard units are used by the people all over the world to weigh and measure things. In earlier days people measured with their body parts. They had no standards. They used handspan, cubit, footspan or stride to measure length. The length of a hand or a foot is not same for all the people. Therefore, size of an object, say a table, would be different for different people. But in the present day the fixed standard units are used for measuring length.

Measurement of length

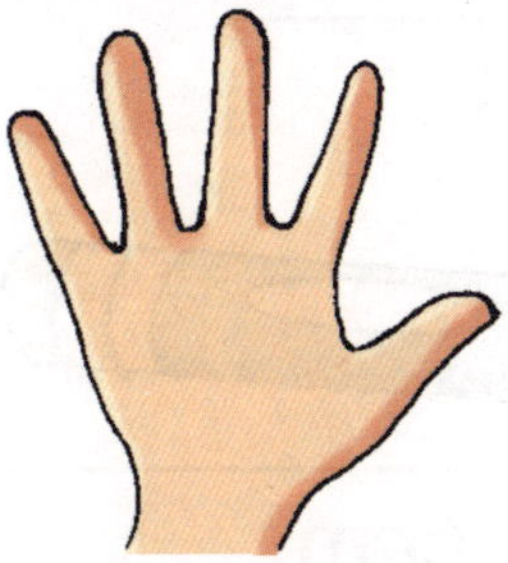

Hand Span

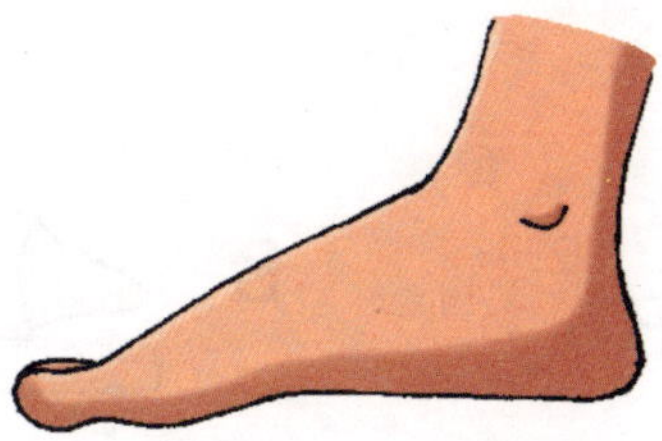

Foot Span

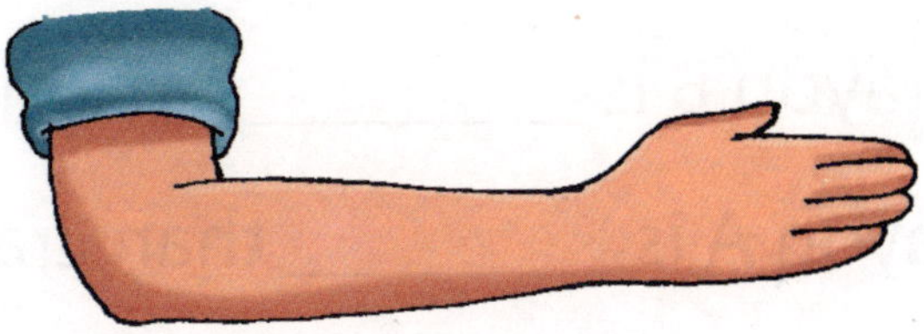

Cubit

ACTIVITY 4

Measure the length of a table using your handspan. Now ask your mother to measure the same table using her handspan.

1. Write the number of handspans counted by you ________
2. Number of your mother's handspans ________
3. Are they both same? ________

The standard unit for measuring length is **metre**. The smaller length is measured by **centimetre** and the longer distance is measured by **kilometre**.

Remember

Metre is written as **m**

Centimetre is written as **cm**

Kilometre is written as **km**

Rulers and measuring tapes are used for measuring length.

ACTIVITY 5

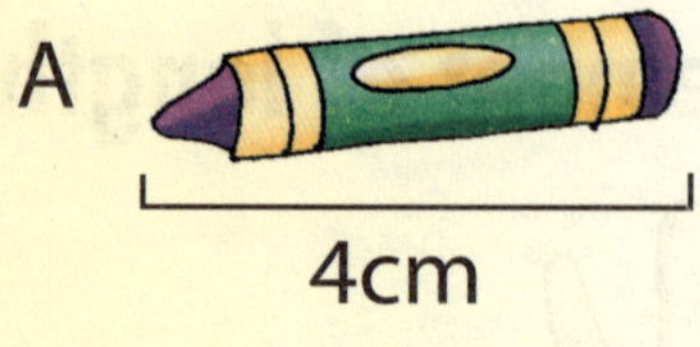

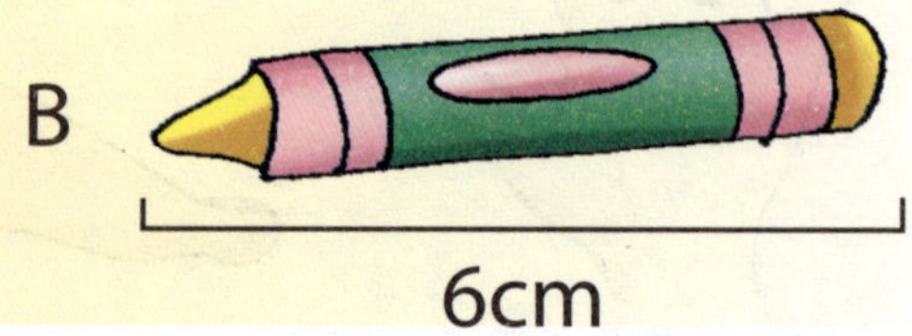

The crayon A is ________ cm long.

The crayon B is ________ cm long.

So crayon A is ________ than crayon B

Measurement of weight

Weight of an object tells us how heavy or light an object is. The weight is measured in **grams** and **kilograms**.

Electronic Balance

Weight and Balance

Remember

Grams is written as **g**, Kilogram is written as **kg**

We use common weight and balance and the electronic balance to measure the weight of things.

ACTIVITY 6

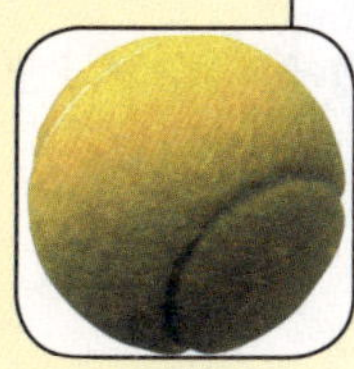

Measure the weight of an football with the help of balance. Now measure the weight of a tennis ball.

Weight of football = ________

Weight of tennis ball = ________

A football is ________ than a tennis ball.

Measurement of capacity

Capacity is the amount of a liquid which a container can hold. Bigger containers have more capacity than smaller ones. In the pictures given below, juice in pack A can fill one glass while juice in pack B can fill six glasses.

Pack B holds more juice. Therefore, pack B has more capacity. Commonly used units to measure capacity are **litre** and **milliltre**. Small amounts of liquids are measured in millilitre and large amounts in litres.

Remember

Litre is written as **l** and millilitre is written as **ml**

Measuring Can

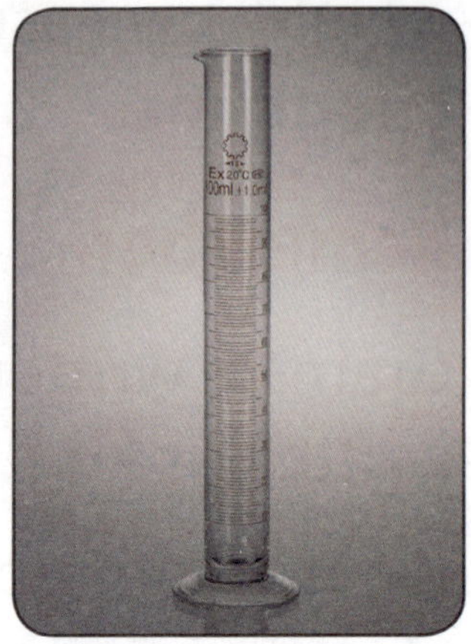

Measuring Cylinder

Measuring cylinders and measuring cans are the instruments used to measure capacity.

Measuring temperature

Temperature is measured to see how hot or cold an object is. It is measured using a thermometer. Temperature is measured in degree Celsius (C°) or degree Fahrenheit (F°).

Remember

The normal human body temperature is 37°C or 98.6°F

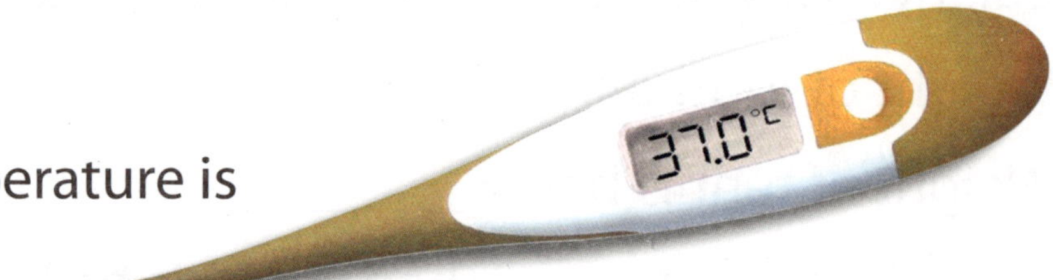

Tharmometer

Measuring time

Time is measured using a watch or a clock. We measure time in **hours**, **minutes** and **seconds**. A day has 24 hours. 1 hour has 60 minutes and 1 minute has 60 seconds.

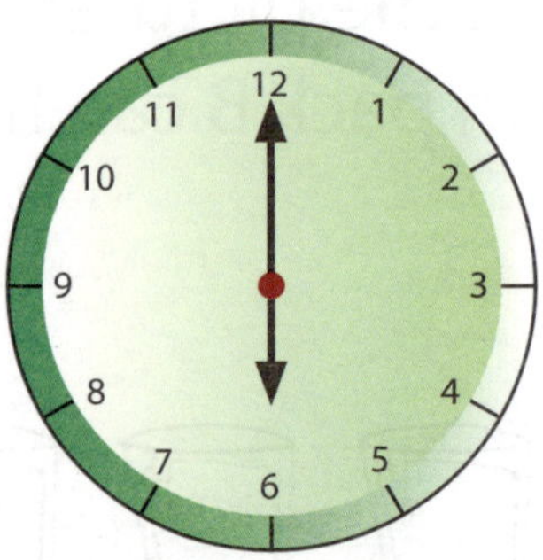

6 : 00

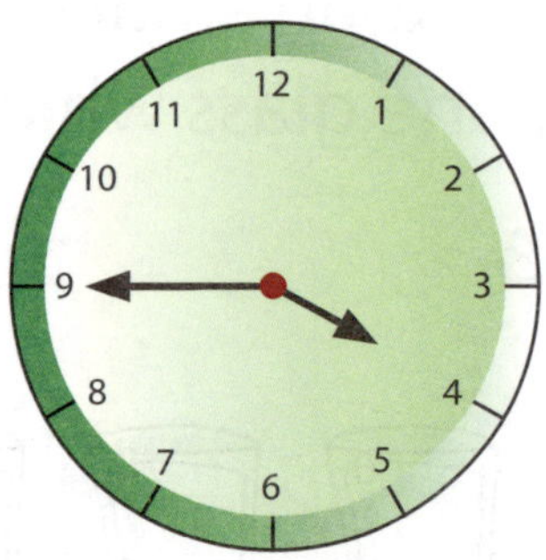

3 : 45

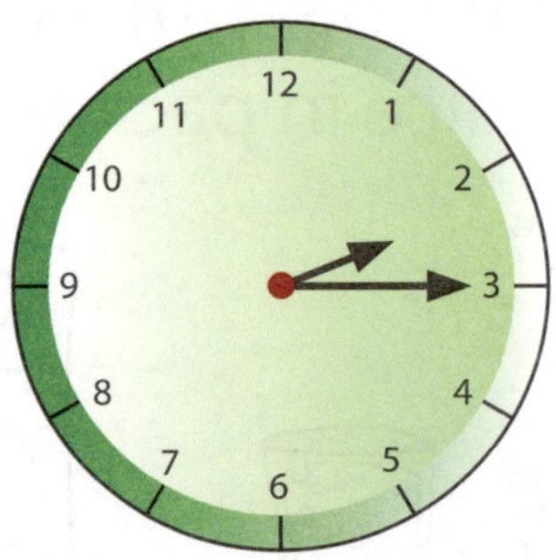

2 : 15

Do yourself

A. Tick (✓) the correct answer.

1. The commonly used unit to measure length is

   a. Metre

   b. Kilogram

   c. Litre

2. In early times, people used to measure lengths with

   a. Handspan and footspan

   b. Measuring tape

   c. Ruler

3. Thermometer is used to measure

   a. Capacity

   b. Temperature

   c. Time

4. Litre or millilitres are the units to measure

   a. Weight

   b. Time

   c. Capacity

5. Which one is correct?

a. 1hour = 60 seconds ☐

b. 1 minute = 60 seconds ☐

c. 60 minute = 1 seconds ☐

B. Answer the following questions.

1. Name two units of measurement used for weight.
2. Name any two instruments used to measure length.
3. What is capacity? Write the commonly used units to measure capacity.
4. What is temperature? Name two units to measure temperature.
5. What is the unit for measuring time?

C. Match the correct unit of measurement with the correct picture.

1. 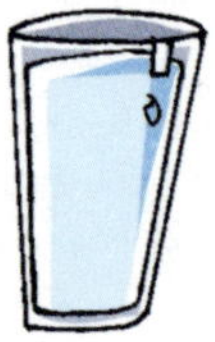 l

2.  ml

3.  Kg

4.  g

D. Measure the length using your ruler and fill the boxes

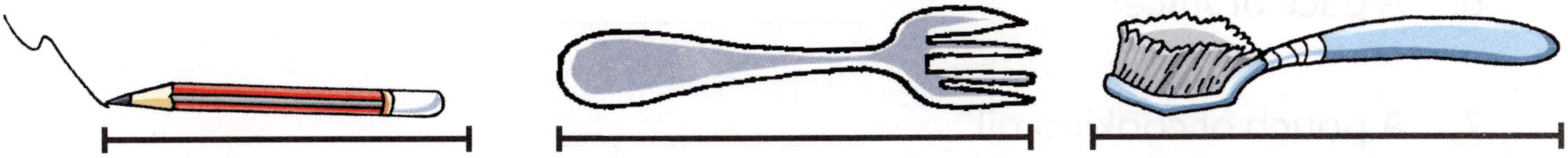

E. Draw the hands of the clock to show the time for the following work you do.

1. Waking up
2. Going to school
3. Coming back home
4. Going to sleep

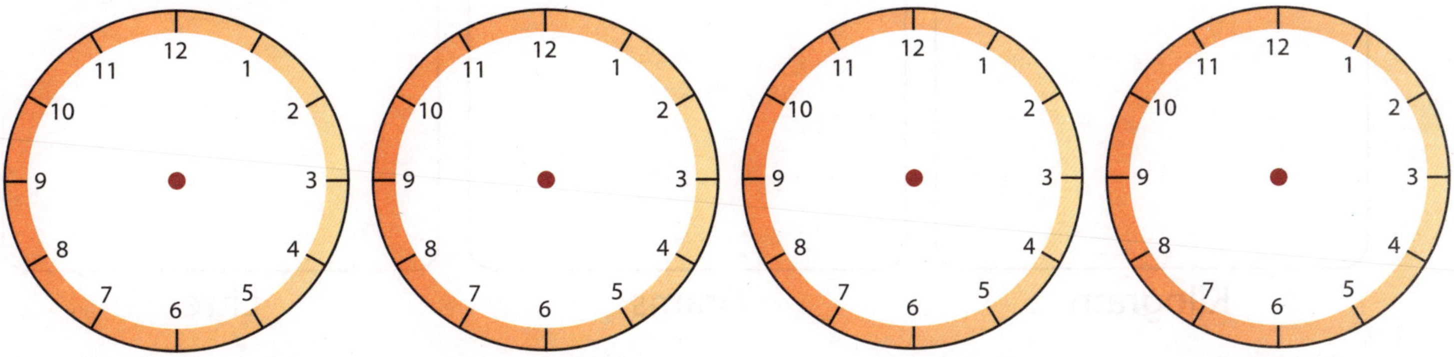

F. Look for these products and check the weight written on them. And then, fill in the blanks with the units shown on the product.

1. A bottle of jam ____________

2. A bottle of ketchup ____________

3. A packet of milk ____________

4. A bottle of shampoo ____________

5. A packet of sugar __________

6. A pack of Juice __________

7. A pouch of cooking oil __________

8. A packet of biscuits __________

9. A bar of chocolate __________

10. A soap bar __________

G. Now that you have learnt much about measurements, draw an object for each of the measurements given below.

Kilogram	Grams	Litre
Celsius	Metre	

Activity time

On an electric weighing machine, find out the weight of your school bag, your science book, school diary, your pencil box and your toy.

11 Force and Energy

Force

In our day to day life, we push or pull things to move them. A push or a pull is called **force**. Force helps us to do many things.

A force can move an object. Force can also stop a moving object. Force can change the direction of an object. Force can change the shape and size of an object too.

Energy

We need energy to do work. Energy is defined as the ability to do work.
If we want to push or pull a table, we apply the energy of our muscles. This energy of the muscles of our body is called **muscular energy**.

Light

Light is also a form of energy. Light helps us to see things. Can you see anything when you enter a dark room? Perhaps not. The moment you switch on the light, you can see everything.

The sun is the main source of light on Earth. We also get light from bulbs, candles, torches and lamps. These light giving objects are called **luminous** objects. The objects that do not give light are called **non-luminous** objects. We can see such objects when light falls on them.

Did you know?

Fireflies are insects which produce light in its body and so they glow.

Luminous Objects

Non- Luminous Objects

Shadow

Light travels in a straight line. When an object comes in the path of light, a shadow is formed. A shadow is always formed on the opposite side of the light source.

ACTIVITY 7

Take a torch and focus it on a nearby wall. Now keep a book in between the wall and the torch. You will see the book's shadow on the wall.

Similarly, our shadows are formed when we block the light of the sun. During the morning and evening time shadows are the longest. It is the shortest at noon.

Sound

Sound is also a kind of energy. Sound is produced when an object vibrates. We hear many types of sounds like the barking of a dog and the tingling of a bell. When we talk we make sounds. Our tongue helps us to make sound.

A Barking Dog

Some sounds are pleasant to hear and some are unpleasant. Unpleasant sounds are called **noise.** Too much of noise is not good for our health. We should always play the television and music system etc at a low volume so that we do not disturb others.

Do Yourself

A. Circle the luminous objects.

B. You hear various types of sounds everyday. Write (P) for pleasant and (U) for unpleasant sound.

1. Sound of a jet plane ☐
2. Fire crackers ☐
3. A song ☐

C. Answer in brief

1. What is force?
2. Name any four luminous objects.
3. Name any four non-luminous objects.
4. How are shadows formed?
5. Write the effects of force?
6. What is noise?

D. Circle the odd one out

1. Bulb Tubelight Diya Fan

2. Sun Stars Hills Candle

3. Sitar Guitar Violin Book

E. Different animals produce different types of sounds. Write the names of animals and the sounds produced by them in the space given.

Animal	Sound

F. Write two examples from your daily life for each situation given below.

1. When the speed of an object changes

   ______________________ ______________________

2. Direction of an object changes

   ______________________ ______________________

3. Shape or size of an object changes

   ______________________ ______________________

Activity time

On a bright sunny day, go to the school ground along with you teacher. Set up a stick in the middle of the playground or in an open space. Measure and record the length of the stick's shadow at different times of the day— in the morning, and noon. Write down the measurement and observation in your book.

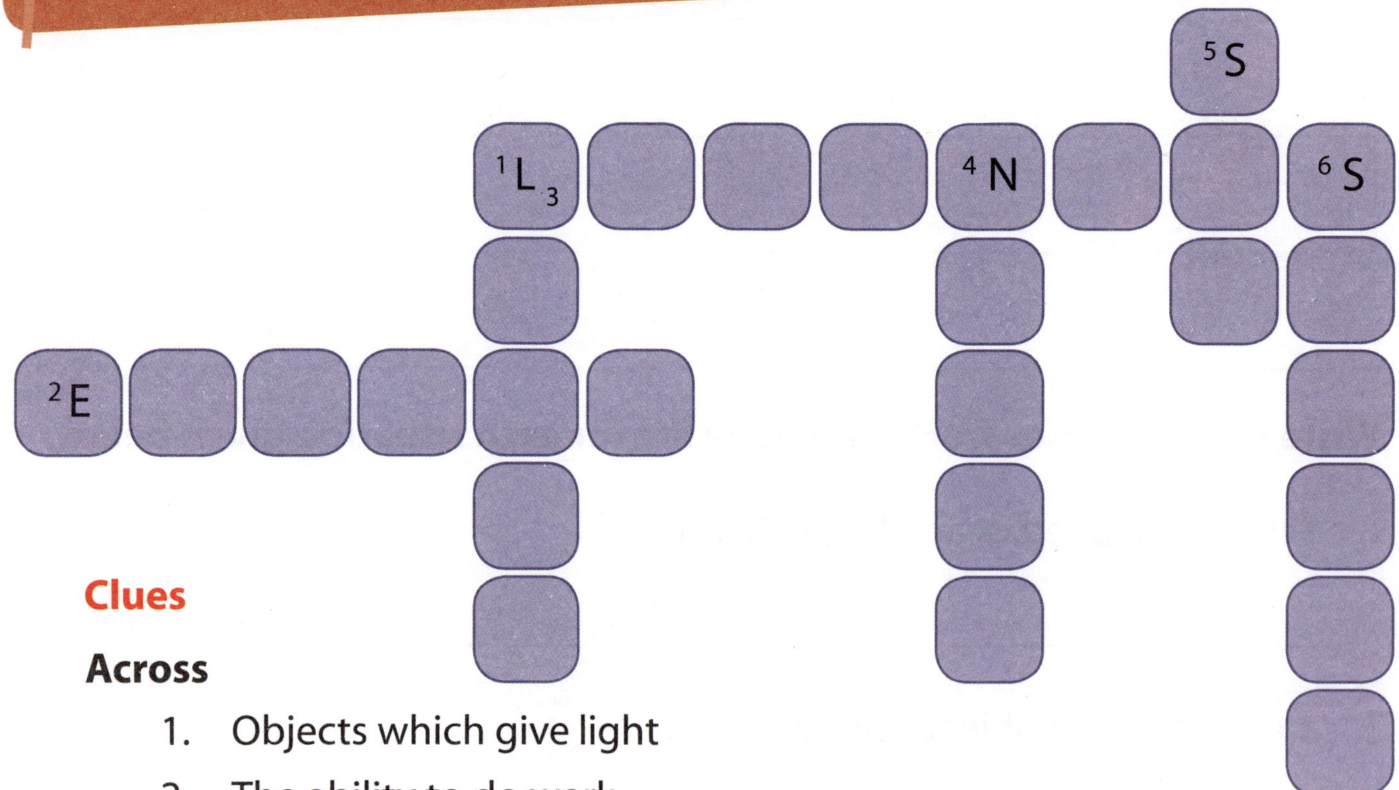

Clues

Across

1. Objects which give light
2. The ability to do work

Downward

3. Opposite of darkness
4. Unpleasant sound
5. A heavenly body around which planets move
6. This is caused when you block light

12 The Heavenly Bodies

We all have seen the sky. The sun shines brightly during the day. The night sky looks beautiful with the moon and the twinkling stars. The sun, the moon and the stars all exist in space. The region of space begins about 800 km above the Earth. There is no air in space. Space is a region beyond the Earth's atmosphere. There are not only the sun, the moon and the stars in the space but many more things are also present like our Earth and other planets. All these are called **heavenly bodies**. Heavenly bodies are those objects which are found in space. Let's learn more about them.

Did you know?

No sound can travel in space. If you tell something to your friend in space, he won't hear it!

The sun and the solar system

The **sun** is a huge ball of burning gases. It gives us heat and light. A **planet** is a heavenly body that moves around the sun. The sun and the eight planets forms the **solar system**. The sun is at the centre and all the eight planets revolve around the sun in their fixed path known as **orbit**.

The eight planets in order of increasing distance from the sun are Mercury, Venus, Earth, Mars, Jupiter, Saturn, Uranus and Neptune.

Solar System

Our Earth is the third planet from the sun. Mercury is the smallest and nearest planet to the sun and Neptune is the farthest planet.

The Earth is a special planet due to the presence of life on it. Life is possible because of the the presence of water, air and the right temperature needed for the growth of living beings.

The planets do not have light of their own. They get the light from the sun and reflect it. Along with planets, stars can also be seen in the night sky. We can easily distinguish between them as stars twinkle while planets do not twinkle.

Did you know?

The sun is in its middle age. It is estimated that the sun is five billion years old and continue to shine for another five billion years.

NOTE

You may remember the order of the planets with this sentence 'My very efficient mother just serves us noodles'. Now take the first alphabet of every word and try to connect them with the names of the planets. 'M' stands for Mercury, 'V' stands for Venus and so on.

The moon

The moon is another shining body that we see in the sky. The moon is our closest neighbour and is 3, 84,400 km away from Earth. The moon is a satellite of the Earth. A **satellite** is an object that moves around a planet. Moon moves around the Earth. It takes 29 days to complete one round. It is smaller than the Earth. This is the reason why objects weigh less on the moon than they do here on the Earth.

Surface of the Moon

The moon has mountains, rocks and craters. Craters are huge holes on the moon. There is no air or water on the moon. Scientists are still trying to find out if water is present on the moon or not.

Moon does not have its own light. It looks bright because it reflects the sun's light falling on it. It has no atmosphere. Hence it becomes very hot when the sun's rays fall on it and it becomes very cold in the absence of the sun's rays.

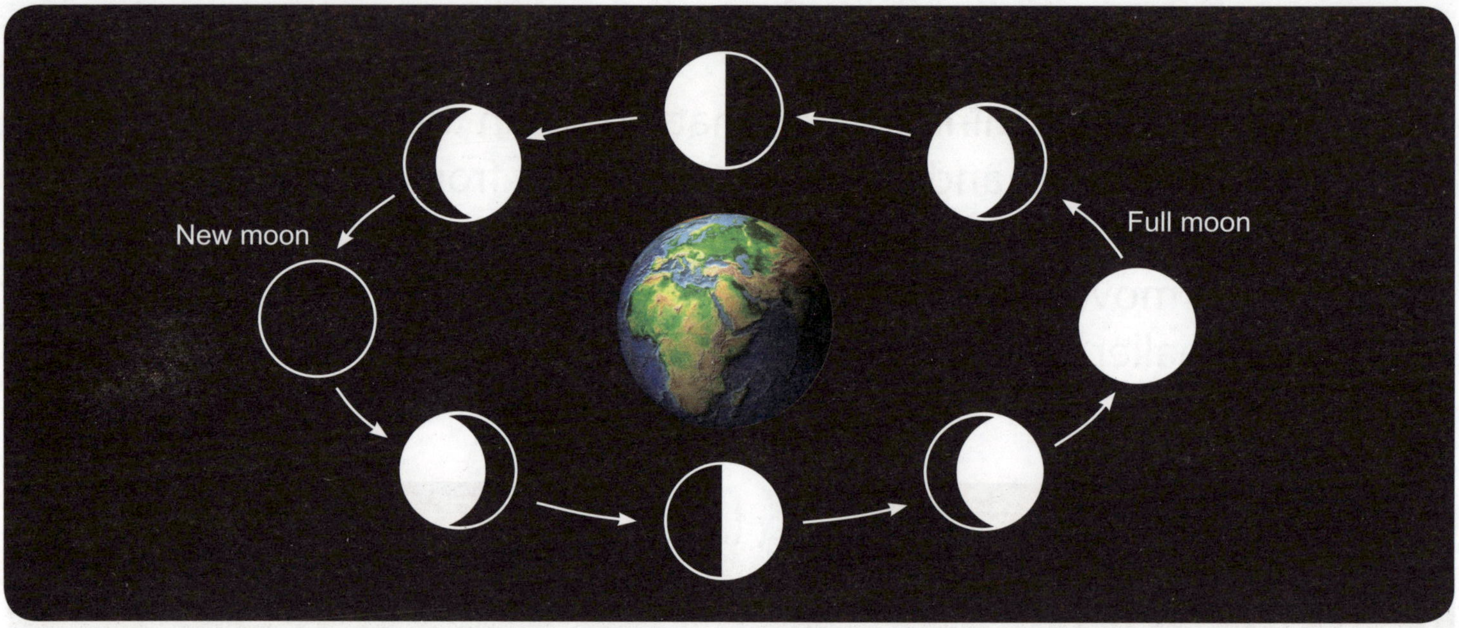

Phases of the Moon

The shape of the moon changes every night. Sometimes it appears circular in shape, sometimes like a half circle sometimes a crescent and sometimes the moon disappears completely. The different shapes of the moon are called the **phases of the moon**.

Stars

You must have seen so many stars twinkling in the sky. Stars are huge balls of fire. They appear very small because they are very far from the Earth. The sun is also a star. It is the star closest to the Earth.

Stars group together to form patterns in the sky. These patterns are called **constellations**. Some of these constellations are the Great Bear and the Orion (the hunter).

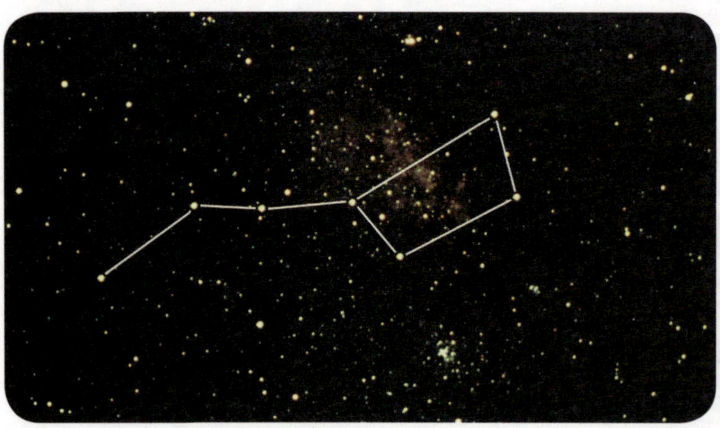
Great Bear

Orion

Space explorations

Scientists always want to know more about space. The scientists who are trained to go into space are called **astronauts**. They go by special aircrafts called **spaceships**.

Yuri Gagrin

Yuri Gagarin was the first man who went to space in 1961 in a spacecraft called Vostok1. The first man who stepped on the surface of the moon was Neil Armstrong. He went in a spacecraft called Apollo 11 in 1969.

Neil Armstrong

Rakesh Sharma was the first Indian to go into space. Kalpana Chawla was the first Indian woman to go into space in 1997. She went again in 2003 in the space shuttle, Columbia. Unfortunately she died on her return journey on 1 February, 2003 when her space shuttle crashed.

Sunita Williams was the second woman of Indian origin to go into space. She stayed in space for six months in 2007.

Rakesh Sharma

Kalpna Chawla

Sunita Williams

Did you know?

Telescope is an instrument used to see heavenly bodies in the sky.

Do Yourself

A. Match the following

Sun	Instrument
Earth	Satellite
Moon	Groups of stars
Constellation	Star
Telescope	Third Planet

B. Find the answer in the word grid using the given clues.

1. A huge ball of fire which gives us heat and light
2. Region beyond Earth atmosphere
3. The planet we live on
4. Huge holes on the moon's surface
5. Heavenly body that moves round the sun

S	U	N	W	B	J	L
P	L	A	N	E	T	V
A	G	P	N	D	K	E
C	R	A	T	E	R	S
E	A	R	T	H	D	J
R	I	O	W	Q	Z	X
L	J	Z	M	O	O	N

C. Answer the following questions.

1. Define space?
2. What is a planet? Write the names of the planets of the solar system in the correct order.
3. What is a satellite?
4. Moon does not have light of its own. Then why does it look bright?
5. What is constellation? Name any two constellations that can be seen in night sky.

D. Tick (✓) the correct answer.

1. The bodies which are found in space are called
   a. Heavy body ☐
   b. Heavenly body ☐
   c. Huge body ☐
2. The nearest star to the Earth.
   a. Sun ☐
   b. Moon ☐
   c. Mercury ☐
3. The natural satellite of the Earth
   a. Moon ☐
   b. Sun ☐
   c. Venus ☐
4. The first man to go into space
   a. Neil Armstrong ☐
   b. Rakesh Sharma ☐
   c. Yuri Gagrin ☐

Activity time

- Observe the different shapes of the moon in the night sky continuously for 15 days. Make a table on a cartridge sheet and draw the shape of moon.

  (Try to start the observation from full moon or new moon.)

	Day 1	Day 2													Day 15
Shape of the moon															

- Few words are missing in the conversation of John and Mira. Complete their conversation by picking the correct word from the stars.

star   sun   Mercury   orbit   third   satellite   eight

John: Hello Mira, Today our teacher has taught us about the heavenly bodies.

Mira: Tell me about something about it.

John: Our solar system consists of the sun and its __________ planets.

Mira: What are planets?

John: Mira, planets are heavenly bodies that revolve round the__________ in their fixed __________

Mira: Is our Earth also a planet?

John: Yes, our Earth is the __________ planet from the sun.

Mira: What is the name of the first planet?

John: The first planet of our solar system is __________

Mira: What is the moon? Is it a planet also?

John: No. The moon is the __________ of the Earth. It revolves round the Earth in its own orbit.

Mira: Thank you John. You have told me such interesting things.

13 Our planet—Earth

We live on Earth. Our Earth is the only planet known to have life on it. The Earth has land, water and air. A large portion of the Earth is made up of water. The Earth is surrounded by a layer of air called the **atmosphere**. Earth gets heat and light from the sun. It is at a right distance from the sun; so the temperature of the Earth is perfect for living beings.

Shape of the Earth

Long ago, people thought that the Earth was flat. Now it is proved that it is round in shape slightly flattened at the poles. The shape of Earth is like an orange. The photographs of the Earth taken from space proves this fact.

Our Earth looks flat to us because we see only a very small part of it.

Movement of the Earth

Spinning Top

Our Earth is moving all the time. We cannot feel the movement because the Earth is moving very smoothly and slowly. We all move along with it. Our Earth shows two kinds of movements— **rotation** and **revolution**.

Rotation

You might have seen a top rotating. A top rotates on its axis. This is called **spinning**. Similarly, our Earth spins around its axis. The axis is an imaginary line passing through the centre of the Earth. The Earth's axis is slightly titled. The spinning of the Earth around its own axis is called **rotation**. It takes 24 hours to complete a rotation which makes a complete day. The rotation of the Earth causes day and night.

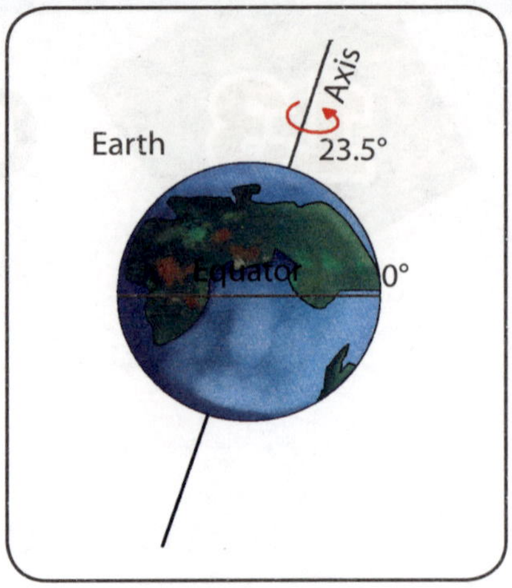

Earth's Axis

Day and Night

When the Earth rotates on its axis, one half of the Earth faces the sun. It is day time on this half of the Earth. The other half at the same the time is away from the sun. So it does not receive sunlight and has night. As the Earth rotates, the lighted part now becomes dark and has night. The part which had night, now faces the sun and has day. In this way, day and night follow each other.

ACTIVITY 8

Aim: To show the formation of day and night

Things required: A globe, a torch, a table and a thumb puppet

Method

1. Stick a puppet on India on the globe.
2. Turn on the torch light. Darken the room. The torch represents the sun.
3. Point the torch light on the side of the globe that has the puppet. This portion of the globe has a day now. The other side of the globe is not getting light. So it is night.
4. Now spin the globe slowly. Notice that the puppet moves out of sight. This means that the puppet is not getting light. Therefore it is night for it.

Outcome: Rotation of the Earth causes day and night.

Revolution

The Earth moves around the sun in a fixed path. This fixed path is called an **orbit**. The movement of the Earth around the sun is called **revolution**. The Earth takes about 365 days to complete one revolution. 365 days make a year. The revolution of the Earth causes changes in the seasons also.

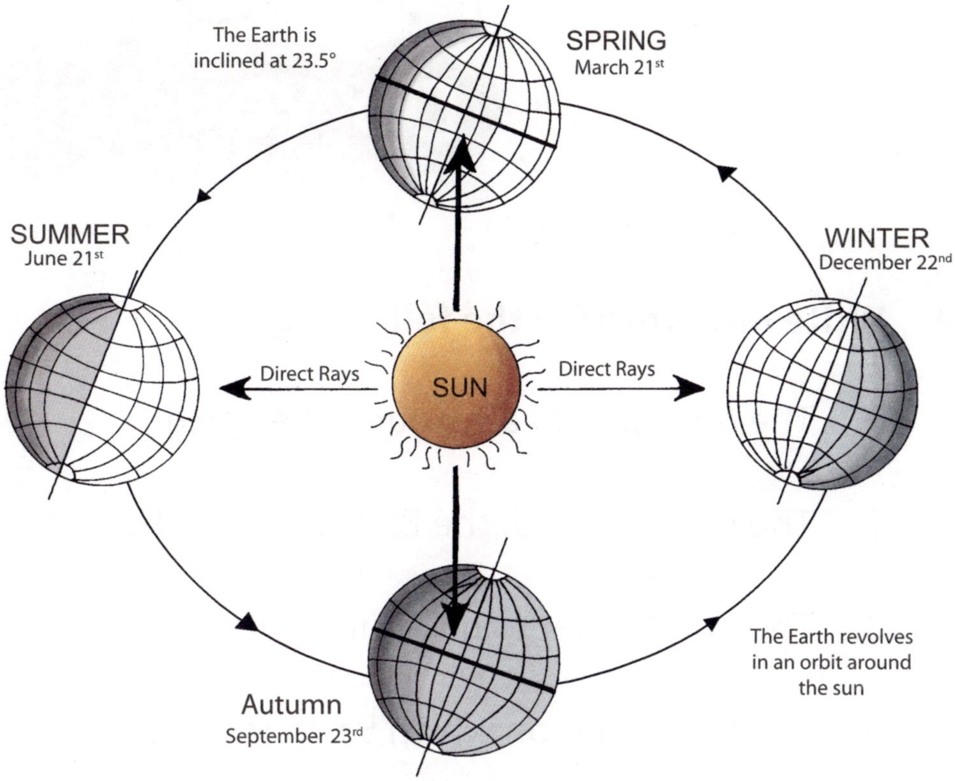

Revolution of the Earth

Did you know?

Earth spins from west to east. So sun appears to rise in the east and set in the west.

The Earth is our home. It is the home of not only human beings but also of different plants and various types of animals. We should not harm any creature on the Earth or even the Earth itself. We should not cut trees or make it dirty.

Some things we can do to preserve our Earth

1. Always keep your surroundings clean
2. Plant more trees
3. Do not use plastic bags
4. Reuse and recycle the items like paper, cans etc.
5. Save energy by saving fuels
6. Do not waste water
7. Use electricity carefully

Do yourself

A. Write one word for the following.

1. The envelope of air around the Earth
2. The movement of the Earth around the sun
3. The only planet to have life on it
4. The fixed path on which Earth revolves
5. It causes the formation of day and night
6. It causes the changes in seasons
7. The imaginary line passing through the centre of the Earth

B. Answer briefly

1. Why does the Earth appear flat to us?
2. What is difference between rotation and revolution?
3. How are seasons formed?
4. What causes day and night on the Earth?
5. How long does the Earth take to complete
    a. One rotation
    b. One revolution

C. Match the following

Seasons	fixed path
Day and night	imaginary line
Axis	rotation
Earth	revolution
Orbit	round

Activity time

Divide the class into four groups. Give each group the task to prepare a wall–magazine on the topic, 'Save Earth and Save Life'.

Reusing waste materials

Don't throw the waste or damaged CDs. You can make beautiful wall hangings and other decorative items using it. Try making some using paints, glitters and stickers.

14 Air and Water

Our Earth is surrounded by an envelope of air. This envelope of air is known as the **atmosphere**. Air is necessary for all of us and all other living beings also. All living things need air to breathe in. We cannot see, smell or taste air. But we can feel it when it blows.

Write two more properties of air other than the ones given.

1. ______________________ 2. ______________________

Composition of air

Air is a mixture of gases. The main gases are oxygen, nitrogen and carbon dioxide. It contains water vapour also. This can be shown by simple activity.

ACTIVITY 9

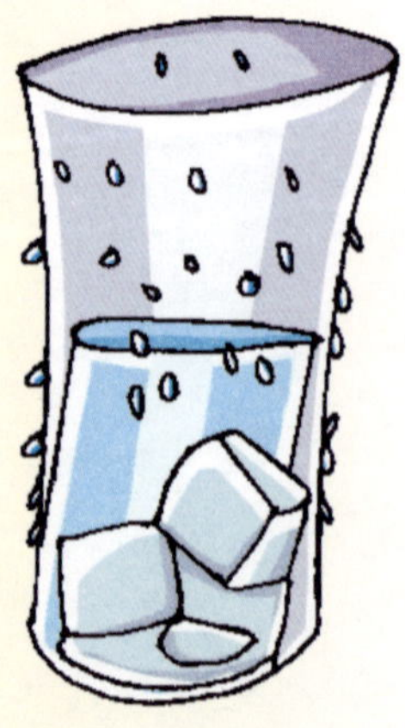

Take a glass tumbler. Fill it with ice cold orange juice or milk shake. After a few minutes you will see water drops on the outer surface of the glass tumbler. The water does not leak through the glass. Then from where did it come from? It came from the air. Air contains water in the form of water vapour. We cannot see it. But when it cools, it becomes water again.

Air contains dust particles and germs also. They stick to our body and we do not even realize it. That is why we should always wash our hands before eating.

Air pollution

When harmful gases and other substances mix with air, it gets dirty. This is called **air pollution**. Polluted air is harmful for all of us. It causes many health problems like asthma and other diseases of the lungs.

We should take measures to check air pollution. Vehicles should be checked regularly. Factories should be built away from residential areas. We should plant more and more trees as trees clean the air.

Air Pollution

Water

Water is one of our basic needs. It is very important for life on Earth. We cannot survive without water. We use water for many purposes in our daily life.

Washing Vegetables

Watering Plants

Bathing

Washing

Drinking

Cooking

Water can be used for fun activities like swimming, boating and water games. Water is the home of various plants and animals.

Water exists in the three forms solid, liquid and gas. Ice is the solid form of water. Water itself is in the liquid form and water vapours or steam is the gaseous form. All these three forms are 'interconvertible' that means it can be changed from one form to another.

The process of changing of water into water vapour on heating is called **evaporation**. Water evaporates from the soil also. Water evaporates from the wet clothes hanging on a clothes line. Plants also release water which vaporises into the air.

Ice (Solid)

Water (Liquid)

Steam (Gas)

Water cycle

We know that all sources of water get water from the rain. But where does this rain come from?

There is lot of water present in different water bodies like rivers, lakes, oceans, ponds etc. This water changes into water vapour due to the heat of the sun. Water vapour rises up and goes into the sky. There it mixes up with dust and smoke and forms clouds. The air is cool at such great heights and so water vapour condenses to form tiny droplets of water.

As more and more water vapour cools into the clouds, the clouds become heavier and heavier. When the clouds become too heavy to hold more water, they come down in the form of rain. The rain water goes back to the seas, rivers, lakes and ponds. From there it again evaporates to form clouds. This process is called the

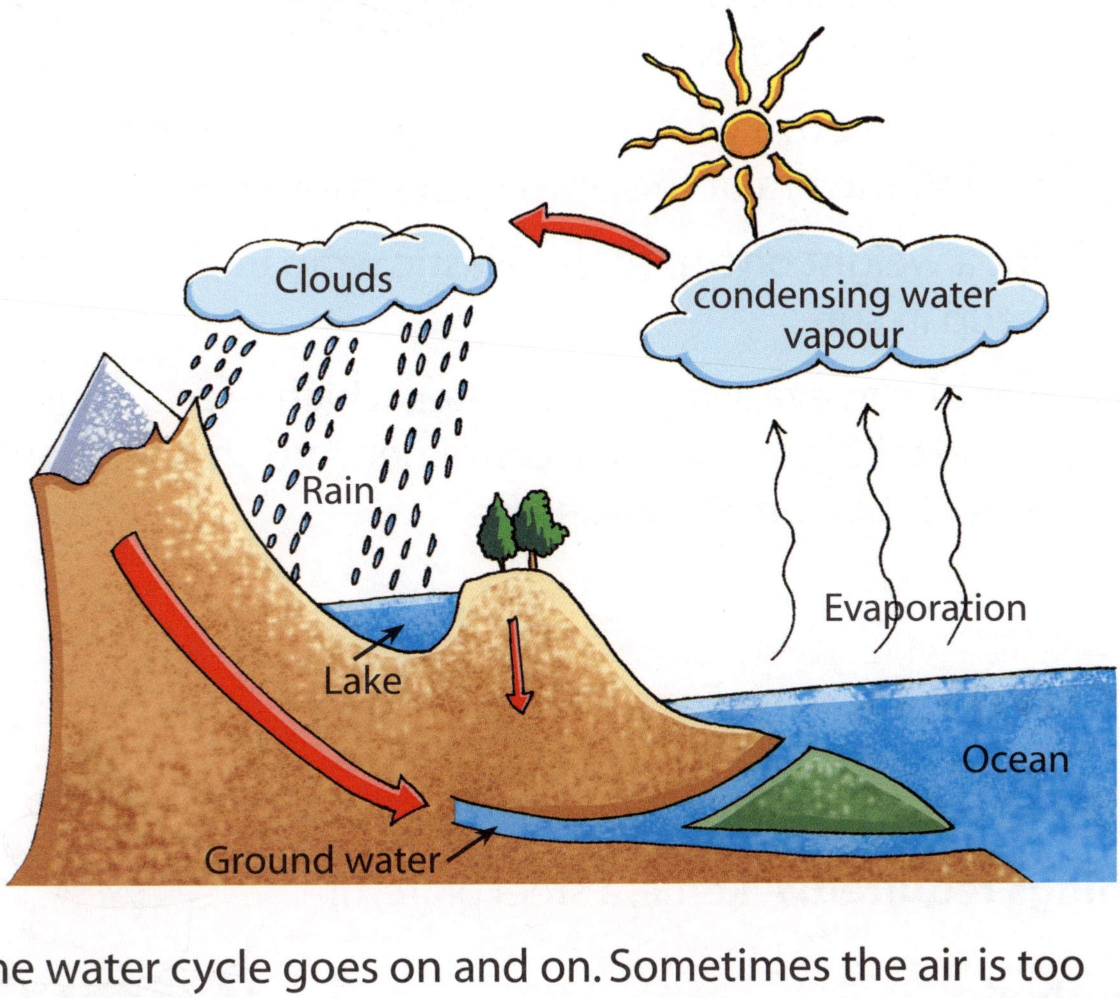

water cycle. The water cycle goes on and on. Sometimes the air is too cold. Then water drops in the clouds freeze to form snow. It then comes down as snow or hail.

ACTIVITY 10

Aim: Making a water cycle

Things required: A glass bowl, a small container, a plastic wrap, a rubber band a weight

Method

1. Take a glass bowl. Place a small container in the middle of the bowl.

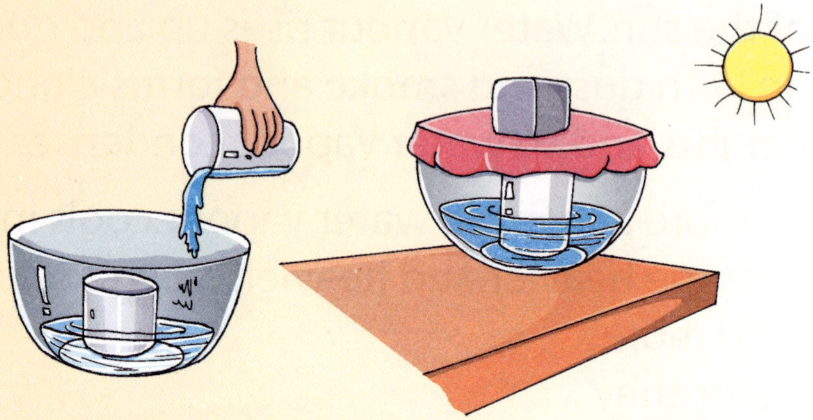

2. Fill the bowl with little water. Take care not to fill the small container.
3. Cover the bowl with a plastic wrap and fasten the plastic wrap around the rim of the bowl with a rubber band.
4. Put a weight on top of the plastic wrap in the centre. Now put the setup in sun.

The heat of sun evaporates the water, which rises, condenses on the cool plastic and falls into the small container. And so, the quantity of water in the bigger bowl remains the same.

ACTIVITY 11

Aim: To show condensation

Things required: A kettle, a steel plate, fire

Method

Heat water in a kettle for sometime. Look at the spout of the kettle. You will see water vapour coming out of the spout. Now hold a cold steel plate in front of the spout. (Be careful as the steam is very hot) What do you find on the plate?

Water vapour cools down and changes to water drops on the plate. The process of water vapour changing into water on cooling is called **condensation**.

On further cooling, water changes into ice. The process by which liquid water changes into solid ice is called **freezing**. On heating, ice changes into water. The process by which solid changes into liquid on heating is called **melting**.

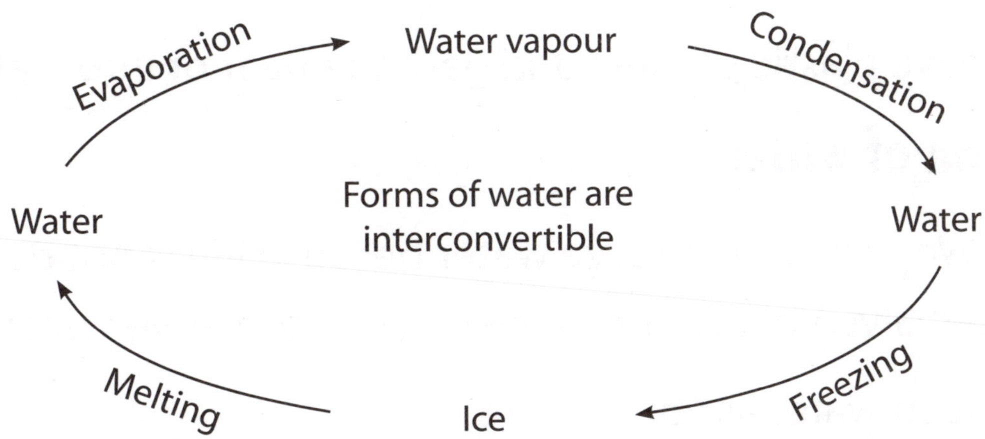

Water pollution

When the sources of water get dirty due to the addition of harmful waste from houses and factories, it is called **water pollution**.

Polluted water is harmful for humans, plants and animals. It causes many diseases like cholera, jaundice and typhoid. Fishes and other water animals die due to water pollution.

We should take following measures to prevent water pollution.

- Factories should treat their waste before releasing it into a river.

Water Pollution

- Do not bathe cattle in water bodies.
- Treat sewage before releasing into rivers.
- Do not leave plastic packets and garbage near or into water bodies.

Conservation of water

Water is life. We need to conserve water because life is not possible without water. Given below are some ways to conserve water.

- Use as much water as you require.
- Do not leave the tap running while brushing your teeth.
- Use a bucket and a mug to have a bath instead of using a shower.
- Wash fruits and vegetables in a bowl and use this water for plants.
- Do not leave any tap leaking. Even a single drop of water is precious.
- Collect rain water and use it for watering plants and washing cars.

Do Yourself

A. Tick (✓) the correct answer.

1. This is an example of solid form of water
   a. Snow
   b. Steam
   c. Rain

2. The process of change of water vapour into water is called
   a. Evaporation
   b. Condensation
   c. Freezing

3. Addition of harmful substances to the environment is called
   a. Pollution
   b. Evaporation
   c. Conservation

4. Water evaporates in nature due to heat of the
   a. Moon
   b. Earth
   c. Sun

B. Answer the following questions.

1. Write the composition of air.
2. What is air pollution? How can we prevent it?
3. Write any four uses of water.
4. What are the three forms of water?
5. What is evaporation?
6. Why is conservation of water necessary?
7. Write any four effective ways to conserve water.

C. Complete the following.

1. Water → [ ] → Water vapour —Condensation→ [ ]

2. Water —Freezing→ [ ] → [ ] → Water

D. The names of a few water bodies are hidden in the word grid. Circle them.

L	G	O	C	E	A	N	S
S	P	R	I	N	G	H	T
D	Q	F	R	I	V	E	R
O	F	J	Z	L	A	K	E
R	A	I	N	K	B	B	A
V	H	D	J	Z	X	C	M
J	H	W	Q	U	S	M	X
W	E	L	L	V	S	E	A

E. Write whether True or False against each statement.

1. Pollution of vehicles should be checked regularly.
2. We should not wash our hands before eating.
3. On heating, water vapour changes into water.
4. Water can evaporate from soil.
5. Water from factories can be released into the rivers without any treatment.
6. We should always bathe under the shower.

Activity time

- Divide the class into two groups. Each group will make a poster on one of the given topics and display them in the class.

  Group 1: Air pollution

  Group 2: Water pollution

- Make a chart showing the water cycle. You can make clouds using cotton.

15 Safety Rules

Rules that prevent accidents and injuries are called **safety rules**. Accidents can happen anywhere at anytime. We can avoid accidents by being careful and by following some safety rules while we are at home, school or on the road.

Safety at home

1. Do not leave your toys, bags, shoes, books etc lying on floor. Someone may trip over them and get hurt.
2. Do not touch electrical gadgets or switches with wet hands.
3. Never play with electrical appliances for you might get a shock.
4. Handle sharp things like blades, scissors or knives carefully. Use them only in the presence of adults.

5. Do not play with match sticks, gas stove or a burning candle.

6. Do not run while going up or coming down the stairs. You might fall down.
7. Do not lean on the railing of the terrace or balcony.

8. Be careful while walking on wet floors.
9. Do not take any medicine on your own.
10. Do not touch hot utensils or boiling water.

Safety in school

1. Do not run up or down the stairs.
2. Do not hit anyone or throw things at anyone.
3. Do not climb on to desks.

4. Do not get into or get down from a moving school bus.
5. Never stand on the footboard of your moving school bus.

Safety in the playground

1. Learn and follow the rules of the games you play.
2. Do not hit others with a bat, a ball or anything else. It may cause injury.
3. Be careful on swings. Wait for your turn to come.

Safety on roads

1. Always walk on the footpath.
2. Use a zebra crossing to cross the road. Before crossing, look to your right, then to the left and then again to your right. If no vehicles are there, only then cross the road or use a subway to do so.
3. Never run across the road.
4. Keep to the left while walking or cycling.
5. Follow the traffic lights.

First aid

Accidents may happen in spite of being careful. If an accident occurs, then the injured person would need help. The immediate help given to an injured person is called **first aid**. Some simple rules of the first aid are to be followed.

1. Keep calm while helping the injured person.
2. Do not crowd around any injured person.
3. Call a doctor or an adult at once.
4. For small cuts and wounds, wash the area with water and wipe it gently with an antiseptic lotion like Dettol.
5. Tie a clean hanky or a bandage over to cover the affected area.
6. If someone has burnt his or her hand, keep the hand under cold water tap until the pain stops.

Do Yourself

A. Tick (✓) the correct option given in the brackets.

1. We should not play with (electrical gadgets/ toys).
2. We should always (run/walk) up the staircase.
3. We should never try to taste (medicine/fruits).
4. We should always walk on the (footpath/road).
5. We should always walk on (right/left) side of the road.

B. Write should/should not in the blanks.

1. We __________ leave our toys, bags and books on the floor.
2. We __________ follow traffic lights.
3. We __________ hit anyone.
4. We __________ stand on the footboard of a moving bus.
5. We __________ play with blades or knives.

C. Answer the following questions.

1. What do you mean by safety rules?
2. Write any two safety rules that should be followed at home.
3. Write any two rules to be followed at school in order to be safe.
4. How can we be safe on the road? Give any three rules.
5. What is first aid?
6. Why should things like toys, bags, books not be left on the floor.
7. Doctor uncle says that we should have first aid kit in our homes. Why do you think he said so?

D. Match the following by unscrambling the given words.

A	B	
We call him in case of injury	DTELOT	
We apply on small cuts or wounds	ANBAGDE	
We apply antiseptic lotion with the help of it	OCDROT	
Cover the wound with	OCTOTN	

E. Let's make a first aid box

We must have first aid kit in our homes. It should be kept in an easy to reach place. Let's make a first aid box.

Take a cardboard box or a plastic box. Keep the following things in the box. You can take these things from a medical store with the help of an adult.

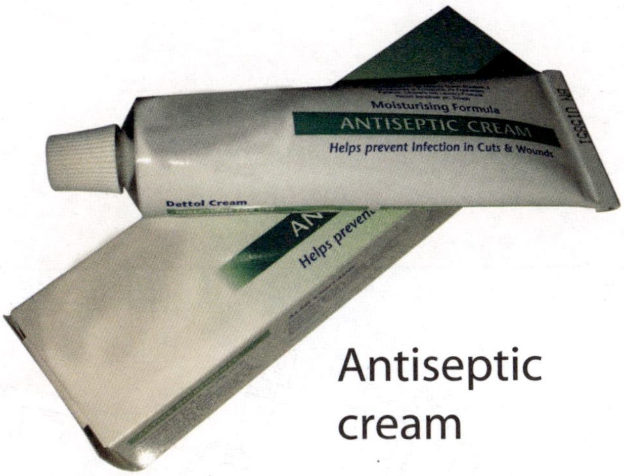

Antiseptic cream

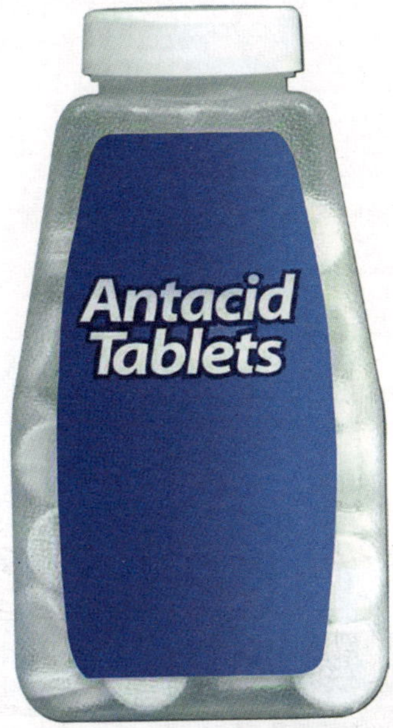

Antacid Tablets

Bandages

Tape

Cotton

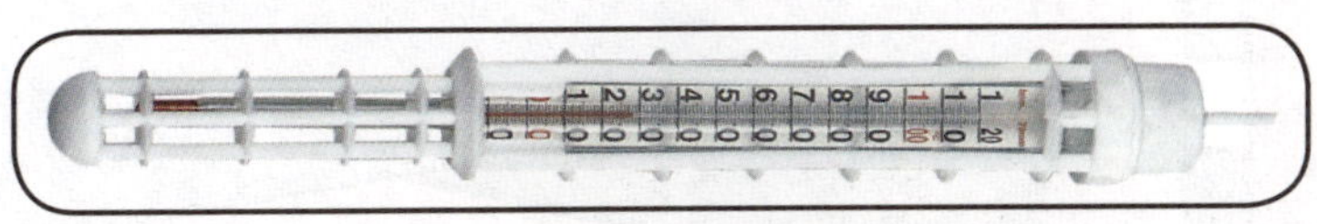

Thermometer

Activity time

- Visit a traffic training park in your town. Find out about traffic signs and rules. Make a list of the traffic signs and their meanings.
- Divide the class into four groups. Tell each group to make a chart on the given topics

  Groups 1: Safety at home | **Groups 2**: Safety at school

  Groups 3: Safety at playground | **Groups 4**: Safety on the road
- Look at the picture given below. There are five things that are wrong. Find out and circle.

TEST PAPER 1

A. Write one word for the following

1. Animals who eat flesh ________________
2. A type of feeding habit in which the animal bites something repeatedly ________________
3. The eating habit of camels ________________
4. Creatures which eat plants and animals ________________
5. Animals living in the body of other animals ________________

B. Write (T) for the statements which are true and (F) for the statements which are false.

1. Loamy is the best kind of soil for plants. ☐
2. Different types of plants grow in different types of soil. ☐
3. Rayon is a synthetic fibre. ☐
4. Dogs have chisel like front teeth. ☐
5. Humans are omnivorous. ☐
6. Vultures and jackals are called as scavengers. ☐

C. Match the following

A	B
Cow	soft, sticky soil
Clay	sticky tongue
Liquid	chewing the cud
Lizard	trunk
Elephant	has fixed volume

D. Answer the following questions in your own words.

1. Define food chain.
2. What is meant by the states of matter? Give an example of each state.
3. What are herbivorous animals? Name any two.
4. Which type of clothes should we wear in the winter? Name the material used to make those clothes.
5. Why are earthworms known as the 'farmer's friends'?
6. What is humus? What is its importance?
7. Write down any two properties of the following
   a. Solids
   b. Liquids
   c. Gases

TEST PAPER 2

A. Write down any four differences between living and non-living things.

Living things	Non-living things

B. State whether the statements are true and false. Write (T) for true and (F) for false.

1. Animals also have sense organs. ☐
2. Non-green plants cannot make their own food. ☐
3. The part of the plant below the ground is called shoot. ☐
4. Stem prepares the food for the plants. ☐
5. Birds have no teeth. ☐
6. Tailor bird sews leaves to make nests. ☐
7. Fishes have lungs to breathe. ☐

C. Answer the following questions.

1. What do you mean by reproduction?
2. How can we make our bones and our muscles strong?
3. Define skeleton.
4. How do plants breathe?
5. Why are leaves important for plants?
6. Write any two special features of birds.

D. Write an example for each

1. Short, hard and horny beak
2. Strong, chisel shaped beak
3. Long, pointed beak
4. Broad and flat beak
5. Strong, sharp and hooked beak

E. Match the following

A	B
Parrot	Scratching bird
Crane	Climbing bird
Woodpecker	Perching bird
Hen	Swimming bird
Geese	Wading bird

F. Draw the beaks of the following birds.

Duck's beak

Woodpecker's beak

G. Draw the diagrams of Taproot and Fibrous root showing their difference in their structure.

TEST PAPER 3

A. Measure the length of the objects and write them down.

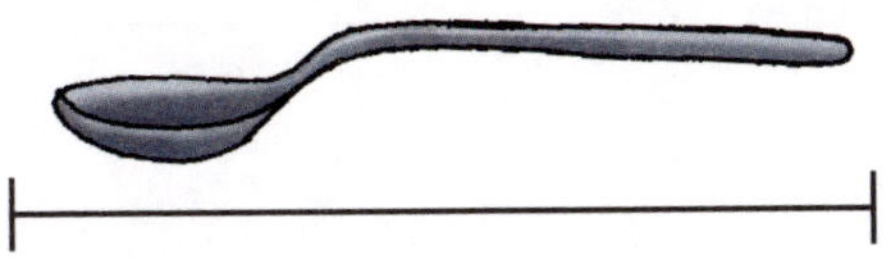

1. ______________________ cm

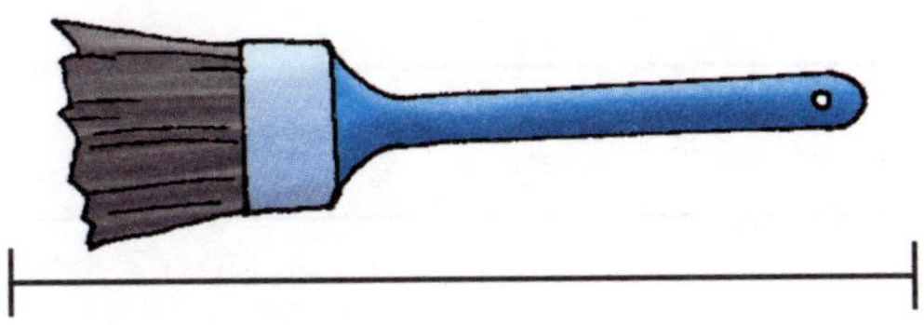

2. ______________________ cm

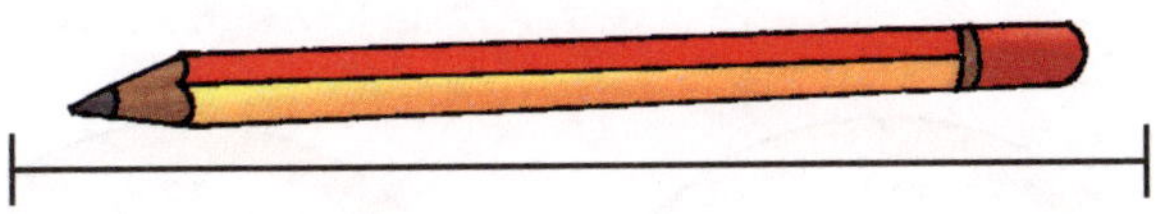

3. ______________________ cm

B. Encircle the correct unit to measure the following

1.	Length of a room	m / Km
2.	Bucket full of water	l / ml
3.	Length of your Science book	m / cm
4.	Weight of a small pack of juice	l / ml
5.	A glass of milk	l / ml

C. Say whether the following statements are true or false.

1. Thermometer is used to measure the capacity of a body. [ ]
2. 2 hours is equal to 120 minutes [ ]
3. 60 seconds is equal to 1 hour [ ]

4. Force can change the shape and size of objects

5. Light and sound are forms of energy

6. Our shadow is the shortest in the morning

D. Complete the given table

Luminous objects	Non-luminous objects

E. Show the given time on the clocks given.

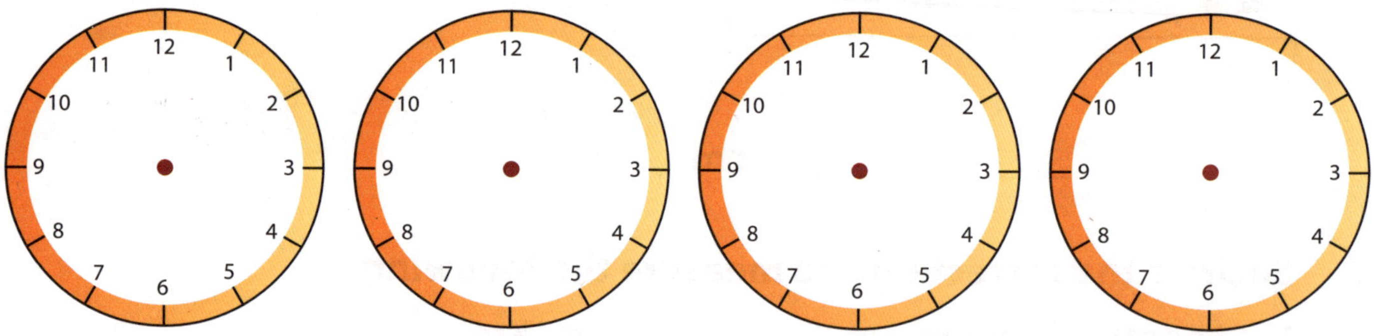

6:45 4:05 9:25 10:00

F. Answer the following questions.

1. Name any two instruments used to measure the weight of objects.
2. How are shadows formed?
3. Write any two effects of force.
4. Name any one unit to measure temperature.

TEST PAPER 4

A. Match the following

A	B
Sun	satellite
Day and night	planet
Moon	imaginary line
Seasons	rotation
Earth	star
Axis	revolution

B. Fill in the blanks with the correct option from the brackets.

1. The nearest star to the Earth is ____________ (sun/ moon)
2. The day and night are formed due to ____________ of the Earth. (rotation/ revolution)
3. The first Indian to go to space was ____________. (Rakesh Sharma/ Kalpana Chawla)
4. The process of changing of water into water vapour on heating is known as ____________.(condensation/evaporation)
5. We should always walk on the ____________.(road/ footpath)

C. Answer the following questions.

1. What is the name given to the stars forming specific patterns? Give any one example.
2. What do you mean by the term 'phases of the moon'?
3. Write any two ways by which we can preserve our mother Earth.
4. Write any four ways to conserve water.

5. Write any two ways to prevent water pollution.

6. What is first aid? Write any two safety rules one should follow in school.

D. Given below is the picture of water cycle. Label the picture in order to complete it.

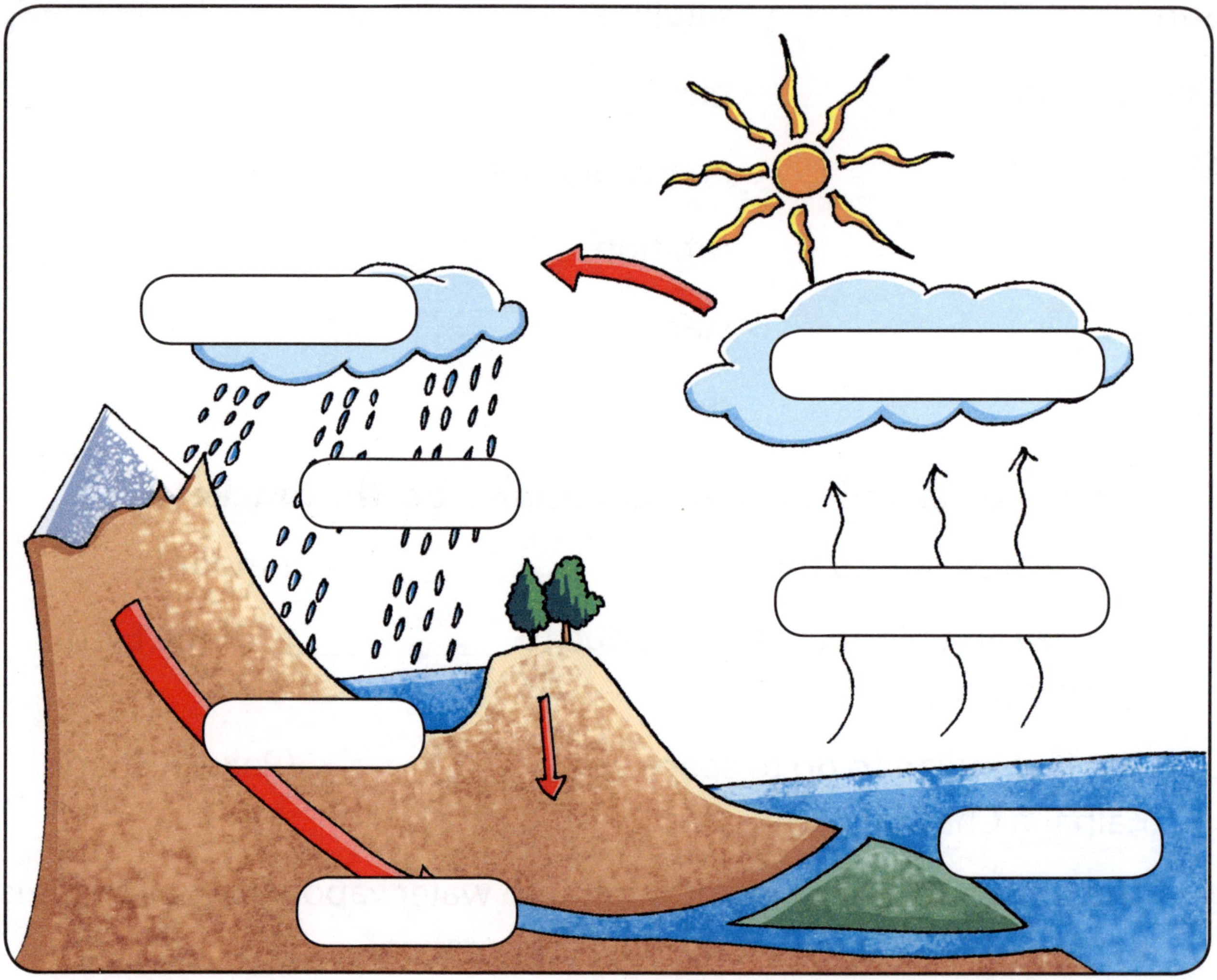